SPAM
A Biography

Carolyn Wyman

A HARVEST ORIGINAL
HARCOURT BRACE & COMPANY
San Diego   New York   London

Library of Congress Cataloging-in-Publication Data
Wyman, Carolyn.
    Spam: a biography/Carolyn Wyman
    p.   cm.
    "A Harvest original"
    ISBN 0-15-600477-1
    1. Cookery (Meat)   2. Cookery (Canned foods)
    3. Canned meat.   4. Spam (Trademark) I. Title
    TX749.W96   1999
    641.6'6—dc21   98-53517

Designed by G. B. D. Smith
Text set in Bookman
Printed in the United States of America

First edition
E D C B A

Permissions and credits appear on pages 133–35, which constitute a continuation of this copyright page.

Ingredients

Shoulder Butt

Loin (Chops & Roast)

Jowl Butt

Picnic Shoulder

Spareribs

Ham

Bacon

Preface

Just saying *Spam* is enough to get most people smiling. Telling people you're writing a book about Spam luncheon meat causes outright laughter, followed by incredulous questions like You're doing *what*? Really? A whole book? What could you possibly say?

I must admit, this was something that initially worried me too—especially considering how much silliness and downright stupidity have been hung on this particular meat hook. If the book was neither to be a mere recitation of Internet inanities nor to be directed primarily at businesspeople, collectors, or cooks, what would it be?

As far as I know, there's never been a book-length study of a single brand-name food. But then, there's never been a brand-name food quite like Spam—one of only a handful of commercial products that virtually everyone knows of and has something to say about. Although this familiarity originally concerned Spam the foodstuff, Spam subsequently transcended its gastronomic origins to become a symbol of American popular culture on a level with Elvis and baseball. Its place in the Smithsonian's National Museum of American History is proof of that.

Spam began its life as cultural icon in the '40s when it became one of the most widely used and widely ridiculed military foodstuffs of World War II. It came into the consciousness of a new generation of

Mother Wyman's SPAM, Baked Bean, and Pineapple Casserole

This was the only Spam hot dish my mother ever made, and it still seems to me to be one of the best. The molassey meatiness of the baked beans and the citrusy sweetness of the pineapple are perfect complements to the salty hamminess and the mushy texture of Spam. The casserole also fills you up in a way that most nouveau cuisine does not. Best of all, it requires no cooking skill beyond the ability to open cans.

> 1 12-ounce can Spam luncheon meat
> 1 28-ounce can baked beans (B&M or
>   other brand with molasses)
> 1 20-ounce can pineapple rings
> 3 tablespoons brown sugar

Heat oven to 350 degrees. Open all cans. Cut Spam into 1/4-inch slices. Dump beans into bottom of medium or large oven-proof casserole dish. Artistically place Spam slices atop beans (like stairs). Cover with pineapple rings. Sprinkle with brown sugar. Bake uncovered 30 to 40 minutes or until Spam is brown and bean juice is bubbling. Serves 4 to 6.

A loving hand guided the future author in the ways of Spam.

Americans when some English comedians whose parents had eaten it as part of their war relief rations wrote a comedy skit about a restaurant with an all-Spam menu. That Monty Python skit, in turn, inspired the Internet term *spamming,* which refers to the sending of unsolicited electronic messages.

As the daughter of a World War II veteran who developed a taste for Spam in the Philippines, I was raised on a regular diet of Spam sandwiches and casseroles made of Spam, baked beans, and pineapple. More recently, as a food writer specializing in the foods of American commerce and culture, I also began to take a professional interest in the product—and even went so far as to name a previous book offering histories of some hundred classics of the American supermarket after my favorite, Spam.

Spam-loving Father Wyman.

The origins of some of the other products in that earlier book were arguably even more colorful than Spam's, but Spam turned out to be the product people were most interested in. And I'm not just talking recipe swaps. It was clear from the stories I heard that Spam had gone beyond the dinner table. It was a concept— nay, a whole culture—worthy of book-length exploration.

My search for the many facets of Spam culture took me by plane, phone, or computer connection from Spam's birthplace in the midst of the American heartland to the typhoon-torn island of Guam, from the tropical paradise of Hawaii to the frigid Alaska tundra. It brought me into conversation with millionaires and race car drivers, with famous poets, artists, and writers, with scientists, newspaper columnists, and prizewinning state fair contestants who told me of Spam wonders, both real and imagined—and, believe me, it's not always easy to tell the difference. In a world where people create recipes for Spam cheesecake and radiology technicians use Spam to mark MRIs, for instance, who would think to question the authenticity of an Andy Warhol Spam can drawing or a recipe for Spam drumsticks favored by General Norman Schwarzkopf? Well, I did, and because I did, this is a work of serious Spam scholarship rather than just another vehicle for spreading Spam myths.

You've no doubt heard the rumors that Spam is made of such unmentionables as pig lips, eyes, and snouts. In fact, for gross ingredients, the generic scrapple and headcheese and the brand-name Armour Star pork brains with gravy have it all over Spam's relatively benign pork shoulder, ham, salt, sugar, and sodium nitrite. Why isn't Jay Leno doing skits about them?

I have several theories. One is that the companies that make these other products are content to let them sit on the backs of grocery shelves gathering dust. Whereas there are no spiffy prime-time television ads showing a modern American family eating Treet, Hormel Foods Corporation still tries to sell Spam in that way.

Another theory is that, despite the contemporary ads, the Spam can design appears frozen in the '30s (or did, at least, until late 1997, when the picture on the label was changed). Then, of course, there's the name, which sounds campy enough to have arisen out of a Batman fight and a little bit crass too, rhyming as it does with the world's most common curse word. And, at a time when pure and natural is all the rage, Spam also screams of being something like—but not quite—ham.

Yet a third theory has to do with Spam's appearance. That perfectly rectangular pink brick looks nothing like any animal in nature and acts little like real meat. Where the quality of regular meat varies from piece to piece, Spam is the same—from the Redwood Forest to the Gulf Stream waters, from 1937 to today. Where real meat spoils, Spam lasts practically forever. Where raw meat requires some cooking skill, precooked Spam can be eaten out of the can.

Some people say Americans are fascinated with Spam because they see it as a sign of our estrangement from nature. I disagree. I think we laugh at Spam for the same reason we laugh at our old high school yearbook pictures and in the same affectionate way. Spam is square—literally *and* figuratively. But like those yearbook pictures, it's square in such a

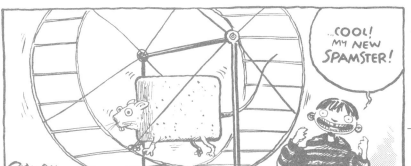

Mixed Media cartoonist Jack Ohman's vision of a Spam animal.

real, sincere, and innocent way as to inspire sympathetic rather than derisive laughter.

Of course, Spam appeals to some people for reasons other than nostalgia. Many like it because it contains salt, fat, and sugar—all the building blocks of good taste. Spam shares these building blocks—as well as uniformity, keepability, and convenience—with many of America's favorite supermarket foods, including Cool Whip, Cheez Whiz, and Bisquick. If sales of any of these foods have dropped (and supermarket scanner data collected by Information Resources of Chicago did show dollar sales of Spam declining about 6 percent in 1997), it's probably not so much because of nutritional concerns or outdatedness as it is because preparing these foods is not quite as convenient as taking out from a modern fast-food hamburger chain. In fact, one of Spam's last major sales spurts occurred in conjunction with a marketing campaign billing it as "the only hamburger actually made with ham."

But Spam's role in American life goes far beyond the kitchen. Because it's so well known and so old, there's hardly an aspect of American life that hasn't been touched by it. This truth was brought home to me one day when I was looking up an article about the Monty Python troupe in an old issue of the *New Yorker* and noticed an adjacent article about the closing of the Lambs, a theatrical club that was the home-away-from-home for Kenneth Daigneau, the actor who gave Spam its name. At the risk of sounding as if I have

Spam gelatin on the brain, I must admit that I have since come to believe that it's possible to view our entire society solely through the lens of this luncheon meat.

Spam, through its recipes, has helped to illustrate women's changing role in American society. Spam, through a strike against its manufacturer, has helped to illustrate the changing role of labor. Spam has played a role in a major art movement and in the blossoming career of a hot new fashion designer. It's played a role in Oscar-winning movies and, some believe, the loss of Native American customs and culture. It's touched controversies over NEA grants and Wal-Mart's impact on downtown business. It has been the dying soldier's last meal and the liberated war captive's first decent one in years. In other words, the depth and breadth of life is all here in the story of Spam.

That may make this book sound

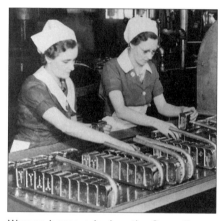

Women have worked on the Spam line since the first day the luncheon meat was made.

serious. In truth, though, probably no product of American commerce has ever generated as much genuine fun and good feelings as Spam has. If this book does nothing but pass along a little bit of that, I will consider my time of Spam study worth all the ribbing.

What do Mickey Mouse and Spam have in common? Not a sharp point or hard edge between them. Just smooth, reassuring curves. That may be one subliminal reason that both are so lovable and endearing.

A Meat Legend Is Born

The story of Spam begins with thousands of pounds of nearly worthless pork shoulder meat. Although the meat is of decent quality, it wasn't highly valued in the meat industry of the 1930s because of the time and trouble it took to cut it off the bone. Consequently, an ordinary employee who suggested that this same meat be featured as the main ingredient in a major new consumer product might have rightly expected to be shown to the door—or at least to a psychiatrist's office. But Jay C. Hormel was no ordinary employee; he was the company's president. And so, in 1937, the pork shoulder meat was spiced, canned, and sold as Spam.

Spam luncheon meat wasn't even Jay Hormel's craziest idea. That distinction would have to belong to canned ham, a product he dreamed up shortly after taking over his father's company. It was 1926, a time when meat companies sold virtually all of their products fresh or cured (a process that extended the shelf life only a short time). That not only put them at the mercy of current pork prices and finite production schedules but also placed their products at parity with every other meat company's. Canned meats did not have these problems, Jay believed, and he was willing to back up this belief with money. Jay sent for German canning expert Paul Joern to help with the technical work and contracted for half a million dollars' worth of advertising to push the ham.

SPAM's Grandfather

Jay's father, George A. Hormel, was appalled. "I can't imagine spending my father's money in any such fashion," he told Jay. "I'm sure you couldn't," Jay replied, "but then, you didn't have a rich dad like me."

George Hormel hadn't started out rich. In fact, his first independent business had been a retail meat shop in Austin, Minnesota. Although it was located in the low-rent district on Mill Street, better known around town as Bourbon Avenue for its lineup of saloons, George astutely predicted that Austin housewives would be willing to dodge the drunks to get quality meat. George opened a tiny packinghouse a few months later, in November 1891, and the following fall his only child was born.

SPAM's Father

Almost from the beginning, Jay seemed a natural businessman. While still a schoolboy, he and his friend Ralph Daigneau paid neighboring housewives two cents a pound for grease they collected from their sinks, only to turn around and sell it to his father's company's soap-making division for twice that price. Later, when a city ordinance required all gasoline cans to be painted red so they could be easily spotted by the fire department, Jay and Ralph bought a couple of cans of paint and parked themselves next to the only filling tank in town. The pair charged fifteen cents a paint job and might have become rich had there been more than fifty car owners in town.

Jay spent his high school summers stuffing sausage and sticking pigs at his father's packing plant. Although he assumed he would be handed the company reins shortly after graduation, George insist-

George A. Hormel's first packinghouse was an abandoned creamery in Austin, Minnesota.

ed that he go to Princeton first. George won the battle but Jay the war by spending most of his study time managing the campus laundry business into profitability. As George put it in his autobiography, "The Dean warned us . . . that at the end of his four-year term, Jay would have a fine laundry and a poor class record." So George brought Jay back to the plant, and when the boy showed up for his first day of work in a business suit, Dad sent him home to change into something more appropriate for unloading hog trucks.

Jay got a bit more seasoning in the service during World War I. Although he went off in search of fame and glory, he ended up at quartermaster depots doing much the same thing in France as he had been doing in Minnesota. Jay made up for the lack of glamour in his assignment by having a romance with a local miller's daughter, which he initiated by letting air out of one of her bicycle tires. He also earned himself a promotion to lieutenant on the strength of his commonsense suggestion that the army could save lots of cargo space by boning beef before shipping it overseas.

Jay Saves the Day

It took something much bigger for Jay to prove his worth back home. It happened one Saturday in 1921 when, searching for some operating figures in the company accounting office, he came across a canceled check for five thousand dollars bearing the notation "transfer of funds." Suspicious, Jay started riffling through more records. By dinnertime he was convinced that the assistant comptroller, Cy Thomson, had embezzled more than a million dollars from the company over the course of several years. It turned out to be $1.18 million.

Nobody had to ask where the money had gone. Everyone in town knew about the fantastic Oak Dale Farms that Cy supposedly had inherited from an elderly aunt, then set about to make the most modern and lavish in the country. In addition to steam-heated swine barns and cattle stalls with fans that blew pesky flies into killing chambers, the farm site in Le Roy had a rooster worth ten thousand dollars, a Cy-made lake, a ten-acre children's playground, a dance pavilion decorated by the same artists who designed New York's Hippodrome, and a fifty-bed hotel for the many tourists who came to see this midwestern Disneyland. Jay had even stayed there once. Cy had been able to get away with it because he was a Sunday school superintendent and a George protégé who supposedly was too dedicated ever to take a day off.

The embezzlement and an already existing three-million-dollar debt almost put Geo. A. Hormel & Company under. But after a meeting with the company's bankers, the needed credit was extended, and the company was preserved to fill its destiny as future source of Spam.

Jay Hormel poses proudly with his company's array of consumer products in 1946.

SPAM's Big Brother, Ham

But first came canned ham. Introduced in 1926, canned ham caught on quickly with hotels and restaurants but proved too big and expensive for the home consumer. What's more, it wasn't long before Armour, Swift, and Wilson were all selling whole canned hams. Jay countered with spiced ham, a unique Hormel blending of chopped ham, salt, sugar, nitrate, and pepper. Again, competitors copied and, again, Jay recognized the need to come up with a product that would be identified solely with his company. His aim was to cut out the competition and, at the same time, to create the kind of steady work that was needed to support a new annual wage plan he had begun in the '30s.

Instead of hiring workers during the peak hog kill in winter and then laying them off when the work slowed down, Jay had instituted a system of paying workers a steady wage year-round. A 1937 *Fortune* magazine article about this and other progressive labor policies at Hormel might well shock those familiar only with the company's labor relations in the 1980s. The article labeled Jay "a Red Capitalist," but the truth was, the *company* would be in the red unless he came up with popular products to keep his workers busy.

Sons of SPAM

All three of Spam inventor Jay Hormel's sons worked at the company that bears their last name for brief periods when they were young, but none went into the family business from which they each now receive three to four million in trust fund dollars annually.

The two younger sons, Thomas and James, live in California. Although both are philanthropists, Thomas maintains a fairly low profile whereas James is well known in the Bay area, most notably for donating half a million dollars to create the James C. Hormel Gay and Lesbian Center at the new San Francisco Library, where his image is included in a ceiling mural of famous gays and lesbians. James became the focus of national attention in 1997 when he was nominated for the U.S. ambassadorship to Luxembourg, an appointment the Christian right attempted to block by publicizing the names of some of the more provocative titles in the San Francisco Library's collection.

Nevertheless, James is a neophyte to the news spotlight compared to his oldest brother, George "Geordie" Hormel II, namesake of the founder of Hormel Foods. Geordie first made headlines in 1951 when he married French ballet star Leslie Caron only days before the premiere of her career-making *An American in Paris*. Geordie met Caron through musicians he got to know after moving to California to play with Lawrence Welk and, later, with his own bebop band. The couple divorced in 1954, the same year that Geordie was arrested on narcotics charges when police found thirteen marijuana cigarettes tucked under the visor of his Cadillac and actress-dancer Rita Moreno bedded down on his couch. He was later acquitted of all charges.

When Geordie remarried two years later (this time to "Texas beauty" Kim

From left to right: James, Thomas, Geordie, and their parents, Germaine and Jay Hormel.

SPAM's Mother

By this time Jay was married to the Frenchwoman who had been the victim of his bicycle vandalism. He and Germaine "Gerry" Dubois lived in a ninety-seven-room, twenty-seven-bath, rambling, red-roofed, French-chateau-style mansion on an estate that grew, in time, to include a guest house, a swimming pool, ceramic-tile-lined horse stables and an exercise ring,

a greenhouse complete with boiler and automatic sprinkler system, and an arboretum of trees and plants from around the state.

Notwithstanding their full staff of bilingual servants, Gerry loved to decorate and cook elaborate beef ragouts and pheasant stews. Everyday family fare included fresh beef, fish, and lamb chops. As

The mansion where Jay Hormel first served Spam.

Wadsworth), Sammy Davis Jr. served as best man. It was Davis's example of a star's very public life that led Geordie to take his musical career behind the scenes. He estimates he wrote almost half of all the background music heard on '50s television shows, and with the money from that he started Village Recorder, "one of the great rock and roll studios of the '70s and '80s," according to *Rolling Stone* writer David Wild. Among those who cut records there: Fleetwood Mac, the Rolling Stones, and Frank Zappa.

Soon Geordie was living next door to Arnold Schwarzenegger, wearing a walrus mustache and a long beard, and dressing in sweat suits and moon shoes. "If you saw him on the street, you would want to give him a buck," a friend says.

Far from being a street person, Geordie today owns what is reportedly the largest home in Arizona—a twenty-bedroom, twenty-six-bathroom Paradise Valley mansion stuffed with consign-

ment furniture, musical instruments, recording equipment, art, CDs, and books. Geordie lives there with his fourth wife, Jamie (a former department store clerk who is forty years his junior), their two daughters, nannies, security guards, recording technicians, environmental researchers, and other assorted hangers-on.

A few years back he sunk a million dollars into an environmentally friendly air-conditioning system only to find out that most people considered its base fuel, butane gas, dangerously explosive. He and Jamie have also been known to round up the homeless and give them showers, clothes, and jobs. When Geordie heard the historic Wrigley mansion was going to be made into condos, he bought it and turned it into a club that, by mid-1997, had

drained him of about eight million dollars. He plays piano there at a Sunday brunch that does not include his father's famous luncheon meat. Geordie may be a Hormel, but he's also a vegetarian and therefore not a fan of Spam.

Geordie Hormel with his wife, Jamie, and daughter Geri.

Thomas Hormel, the second of three sons born to Jay and Gerry between 1928 and 1933, put it, "With chefs in the house, you wouldn't be inclined to have them prepare canned meat."

But, Thomas said, his mother would often consult with Hormel chef Jean Vernet, also a French import, over "the contents of company products." And guests to the Hormel home grew used to serving as test subjects for Jay's brainstorms. Thomas remembers one cocktail party where the as-yet-unnamed Spam was served cubed on toothpicks as an hors d'oeuvre.

The first products Jay introduced for the consumer market seemed to come out of his privileged, bicultural personal life. They included the premium-priced Hormel whole chicken in a can, introduced in 1929, and a line of gourmet soups featuring such varieties as jellied consommé, consommé madrilene, French-style onion, and tomato bretonne (or bean soup, as even *Fortune* magazine saw the need to explain to its upscale readers). The onion soup was based on Gerry's recipe and in advertisements was eaten by a woman in a low-cut gown and a man in a tuxedo. Meanwhile many Americans were standing in soup lines. No wonder sales were dismal.

SPAMterfuge

Like Hormel chili and Dinty Moore beef stew, both of which were intro-

Hormel chef Jean Vernet.

duced in 1935, Hormel's first pork luncheon meat, the predecessor to Spam, came closer to Depression-era reality. Since the luncheon meat debuted in six-pound cans, its main purchasers were not home consumers but butcher shops and delis that opened the cans, put the loaves in their refrigerator cases, and sliced them to order. That created a new problem.

Once opened, one luncheon meat looked pretty much the same as any other. Although the pork shoulder in Hormel's luncheon loaves was filet mignon compared to the lips, ears, tongue, and, yes, even pig snouts competitors put in the ones they came out

with following Hormel's success, consumers couldn't tell the difference by their appearance. As a result, Hormel began losing business to these cheaper products, in some cases because of meat manager hocus-pocus that resulted in their being sold as Hormel luncheon meat.

If Jay was slow to get the message when competitors ripped off his canned ham and spiced ham, he had it now: If he wanted Hormel luncheon meat to succeed, he was going to have to sell it in consumer-sized cans bearing a trademarkable name.

The Battle against Loose Juice

The group of technical people who were gathered to work on the project decided on a twelve-ounce size (enough to feed a family of five dinner, with leftovers for sandwiches the next day) and a rectangular shape (so that the meat could easily fit on a slice of bread). Since no such can already existed, team member Julius A. Zillgitt went down to the Square Deal Grocery store in his Model A Ford and found a can of Mazola oil that was too large but exactly the right shape. Then he went to the tin shop, dumped the oil out, put twelve ounces of water in, cut the can down to the right height, filled it with meat, put a cover on, soldered it, and processed it.

The result? Eight ounces of solid rock meat and four ounces of worthless liquid. Thus began what became known in Spam circles as the battle against loose juice. But from the perspective of canning history it was just the latest skirmish. Scientists had had the experience of seeing cell walls break down and give up fluids under the heat of canning

since the late 1790s, when Napoleon offered 12,000 francs (about $250,000 in today's U.S. currency) to anyone who could figure out a way to keep his soldiers from being felled by food poisoning. Hormel itself had encountered many of the same problems while developing its Flavor-Sealed canned ham.

Adding salt, finding the proper cooking time, and sucking the air out of the can to create a vacuum had done the trick for Flavor-Sealed. But twelve ounces of pork luncheon meat reacted differently, and any number of factors—"the can, the solder, the seam, the fill, the mix, the cure, the age of the pig, the feed of the pig, the cast of the moon"—could "cause too much precipitation of juice from the meat," lamented a 1943 article in the *Squeal,* the Hormel company newsletter. The solution that Zillgitt and the other Spam scientists eventually discovered involved mixing the meat in a vacuum and depositing it into cans in precisely the right way.

Spic or SPAM?

Even after Zillgitt and his colleagues had cooked the loose juices' goose, though, the product sat for two years waiting for the right name. The delay is understandable when you hear some of the entries in a company naming contest Jay launched. *Brunch* was an early favorite. Inspired by Sinclair Lewis, a native Minnesotan who had used the quite-new word *bruncheon* in his 1915 novel *The Trail of the Hawk,* the name

HERE'S THE STORY OF TASTY **SPAM** PURE PORK SHOULDER BLENDED WITH HAM; MADE BY US AT AUSTIN, MINN., WE'VE *FLAVOR-SEALED* THE GOODNESS IN!

may have been nixed because the novel's hero comes down with typhoid fever immediately after eating a fashionably late morning meal.

Jay and company also apparently considered the name *Spic.* The word was already a derogatory term for Hispanics but in this case was more likely derived from an Old English term for fat or grease. Happily, Hormel decided to reserve the name for a shortening product.

Spam still had no name in late 1936 when, as legend has it, Jay decided to throw a New Year's Eve party at which guests earned a drink for each entry they made in the naming contest. "Along about the fourth or fifth drink they began showing some imagination," Jay said later. The

A Spic label mock-up from the Hormel archives.

reward for suggesting the now-famous name—a hundred dollars—went to Kenneth Daigneau, the visiting actor-brother of Hormel Vice President Ralph Daigneau (Jay's former partner in grease-gathering).

Like *brunch, Spam* is a portmanteau word—a word that is a combination of other words in both form and meaning. Most company sources say *Spam* comes from *spiced ham.* Another theory, that it comes from *shoulder of pork and ham,* could help to explain the product's lack of what are traditionally

thought of as spices. However, a *Squeal* article written in the early '40s says the original Spam contained no ham; Jay only added it later to live up to the expectation created by the name. It also says that Jean Vernet came up with Spam's cure and blend. So the Spam recipe actually came from a French chef on the order of Julia Child!

The historic spot where Spam got its name.

His Best Performance?
At SPAM's Naming Party

The man who named Spam was an actor who, after learning the ropes with stock companies across the country, graduated to leading or straight-man roles in Broadway flops and wildly melodramatic radio dramas. Kenneth Daigneau's acting career may have reached its nadir when he accepted a regular part in *Stella Dallas,* the radio continuation of a Barbara Stanwyck movie about a mettlesome mother of little "school learnin'" whose daughter, Lolly-Baby, marries above her. In one memorable episode, Lolly-Baby is abducted by a sheik, and Stella comes to her rescue by piloting a submarine through the Suez Canal.

Daigneau's tiny 1948 obituary in the show business trade newspaper *Variety* mentions his age (fifty) and the cause of his death (heart attack), but not his most lasting contribution to world culture: giving Spam its name.

SPAM Day

After some time to gear up production and promotion, Spam was registered as a trademark on May 11, 1937—its official birthday. (Nineteen thirty-seven also witnessed the birth of Jane Fonda, Daffy Duck, the Appalachian Trail, Kraft macaroni and cheese dinner, and the Golden Gate Bridge, which is 13,440 Spam cans long.)

Spam luncheon meat was a tough sell at first, partly, according to former Hormel public relations chief Stuart H. "Tate" Lane, because

WHAT MEAT NEEDS NO REFRIGERATION?

SPAM

A NEW HORMEL MEAT

Two of many early Spam knockoffs.

housewives of that era had "been raised by their mothers to believe that if you ate meat that had not been refrigerated, you'd be sick the next day." But it quickly picked up in popularity. One measure was in the number of monosyllabic competitors it spawned. Treet, Mor, Prem, Snack, Tang, and more than a hundred others came on the market within the next two years, most leaving just as quickly.

Jay Hormel had finally created the unique consumer product for which he had long searched, and in the process he had helped to raise the value of a hog, supply an affordable protein source to Depression-era families, support Hormel's progressive new wage plan, and begin the transformation of a meatpacking company into the manufacturer of brand-name food products that it is today.

The February 1, 1938, issue of the *Squeal* confirmed Spam's early success when, with a nod to *Time*'s Man-of-the-Year award, it named the luncheon meat the company's best new development of 1937:

Careful readers of this chapter should have no trouble answering the history question on card 403 of the original blue box or Genus (general knowledge) edition of Trivial Pursuit.

Size? Look at the invoice records. Importance? Yes, sir. Significance? It is another contribution to the business of adding value, convenience and attractiveness to the farmer's product so that his hog is more in demand by Mrs. American Housewife.

Ingeniousness? Did you know how difficult a mechanical feat it was to put a product in a small can in such a manner that it will keep fresh and wholesome for a long, indefinite period of time?

Pleasure? We expect chief concurrence in our nomination from the tens of thousands who have eaten Spam roasted per directions on the can.

TIME *(to eat)*

MEAT *of the* YEAR

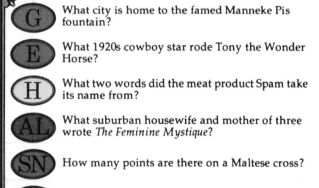

G — What city is home to the famed Manneke Pis fountain?

E — What 1920s cowboy star rode Tony the Wonder Horse?

H — What two words did the meat product Spam take its name from?

AL — What suburban housewife and mother of three wrote *The Feminine Mystique*?

SN — How many points are there on a Maltese cross?

SL — What's men's par on a 455-yard golf hole?

403

SPAM TOWN, U.S.A.

"**H**ormel's got his feet sticking out the window again." That's the way generations of schoolchildren have described the smoked pork aroma that pervades the streets surrounding the meatpacking plant in Austin, Minnesota—much as Hormel Foods Corporation dominates this southeastern Minnesota town of about twenty-three thousand.

George Hormel (the name originally rhymed with *normal,* although now all but old-time Austinites put the accent on the second syllable) had become familiar with this little

Hormel stockholders at the company's 1959 annual meeting.

town near the Iowa border when he was a young wool and hide buyer because it was the northernmost point on his sales route. It became one of his favorite places to spend weekends, especially with a turn-of-the-century singles group called the Toboggan Club.

Today about sixteen hundred Austin residents work for the meatpacking company George founded, which changed its name from Geo. A. Hormel & Company to Hormel Foods Corporation in January 1993. Considered along with the additional thousand people who work at Quality Pork Processors (the company created to handle butchering operations for Hormel after a strike in the mid-'80s), the local farmers who supply most of the 4.2 million

hogs slaughtered there annually, and the late-November dividend checks that local merchants count on to boost holiday sales, it's not surprising that many Austin adults call the town's smoked pork aroma "the smell of money."

But the influence of Hormel Foods goes well beyond paychecks. The corporation and the foundation that controls nearly half its stock helped build the town's hospital, library, and senior citizens center, and they continue to support community organizations to the tune of several million dollars annually. First graders at some local schools have even learned to count from handouts picturing the company's products. Is it any wonder that a can of Spam made the time capsule placed in the

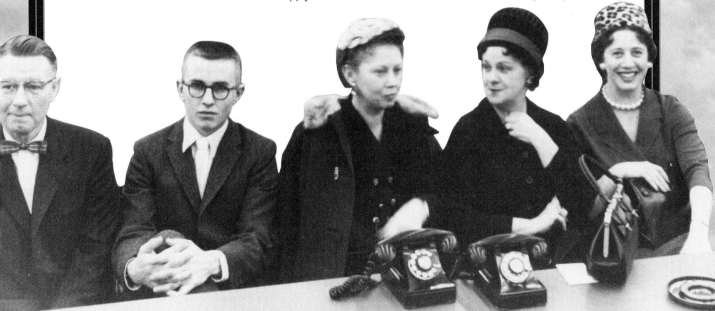

HORMEL PLANT — AUSTIN, MN

cornerstone of the city's First Congregational Church?

This is also a town where Spam gets its own supermarket aisle sign and is the featured ingredient in a specialty sandwich at the country club. Nobody will laugh at you if you order it, either. (Of course, this is also a town whose visitors guide lists Kmart under dining establishments.)

Next to the Spam Jam, the Miss Minnesota Pageant, and the National Barrow Show (the largest show in the world devoted to prize pre-Spam), the biggest event of the year in Austin is Hormel Foods' annual meeting in late January. It's one of

the best-attended annual meetings in the world, too. In part, this is because of the large number of Hormel Foods stockholders living in Austin; in part, because of the com-

pany's symbiotic relationship with the town; and in part, as former Hormel President I. J. Holton once suggested, because of "how damned dull it can get out here in the middle of winter."

For whatever reason, nearly two thousand Austinites typically pack the high school auditorium to vote on the company's directors and hear its executives talk about the past year. Former Austin Convention and Visitors Bureau executive director Debbie Vorpahl says it's "like a town meeting." It's also a social event before which the town's hair salons have to squeeze you in. People commonly arrive an

hour early to see and be seen.

At least that's the way it was until members of Local 9 of the United Food and Commercial Workers Union walked out of Hormel's Austin plant in 1985 in a dispute over wage and benefits

CEDAR RIVER

AUSTIN MINNESOTA

Points of Interest on the Austin SPAM Trail

Hormel Foods' Austin plant, 500 NE 14th Ave., and corporate office, 1 Hormel Place. 507-437-5611. Hormel Foods no longer offers plant tours to the general public. But people who visit as part of a bus group of forty or more can schedule a visit to the company's archives, sometimes even in conjunction with a concert by the Spamettes, a local singing group with an all-Spam repertoire. To inquire about setting up a tour, call the Austin Convention and Visitors Bureau at 1-800-444-5713.

Hormel Foods and Spam Historical Center, OakPark Mall, intersection of Highway 218 North and Interstate 90. 507-437-5100. Open regular mall hours; no admission fee. Originally called Hormel's First Century Museum, this center opened as part of the company's celebration of its centennial anniversary in 1991 and was supposed to close at the end of that year. However, the crush of visitors convinced Hormel to leave it open. In 1998, the company renamed it, gave it a new Spam can facade, and replaced the slowest of the exhibits (pictures of Hormel CEOs and architectural renderings of its plants) with Spam artifacts—old and foreign cans, a map marked with all the countries where Spam is registered as a trademark, and a continuously running video of Spam TV ads. Other display cases feature samples of (mostly defunct) Hormel products, including a tube of dog dessert and a can of luncheon tongue ("It speaks for itself," a customer once suggested as an ad slogan), and memorabilia from the Hormel Girls, a group of ex-GI women who traveled the country singing and marketing Hormel foods. There's also quite a bit about the embezzlement scheme that nearly ruined the company in 1921—but nothing about the even more newsworthy strike in the mid-'80s. The censors apparently overlooked the display case on early pig processing, which includes knives, a huge hypodermic needle, and a photograph of the smiling "hog kill gang."

George A. Hormel home, 208 NW 4th Ave. 507-433-4243. Tours by appointment. Just before George Hormel's retirement to California in 1927, he and his wife, Lillian, donated their stately Italianate home in Austin to the YWCA. Although the house is no longer affiliated with the Y, single women still live on the second floor, which is why visitors cannot see the Hormels' bedrooms or the bed Jay slept in as an adult (moved here from his former home) except during a late-November fund-raising open house. For that reason, only architecture buffs should probably go out of their way.

Jay C. Hormel Nature Center, 1304 NE 21st St., a quarter of a mile north of Interstate 90. 507-437-7519. Sometime in the '30s Jay and Germaine Hormel set aside part of their property to be a living museum for trees and plants from around the world, including every tree known to grow in Minnesota. This part of their estate has since become a nature center with

Jay Hormel's Spam-like tombstone.

more than seven miles of trails open to roaming. Jay's ninety-seven-room mansion now houses the Gerard residence for emotionally disturbed children and is not open to the public.

Oakwood Cemetery, 1800 NW 4th St. 507-433-3304. Look for the tallest monument and you'll find the graves of George, Jay, and many other Hormels.

Sterling Drug, 1417 SW 1st Ave. 507-433-4586. The postcard rack in the back of the store includes several cards featuring the Hormel plant. To get the full Spam postal experience, mail the cards at the instore post office there and ask the clerk to use the Spam Town, USA, postage meter.

The Old Mill, Holiday Inn, Jerry's Other Place, Kenny's Oak Grill, Steve's Pizza, Tolly's Time Out Restaurant & Lounge, Watts Cookin', and some half dozen other eateries. The largest single group of restaurants outside Hawaii to feature Spam on their menus.

Individuals with flexible schedules would be smart to plan their visit to Austin to coordinate with the Spam Jam, a country-fair-like event held every Fourth of July weekend. (See Chapter 8 to learn more about it.)

A-3

Greetings from AUSTIN

THE SWINE CAPITOL OF THE WORLD

MINNESOTA

SPAM TOWN USA · AUSTIN, MN

SPAM™ TOWN USA

SPAM®

T-shirts, the city Web site, and promotional literature that the Convention and Visitors Bureau hopes to use to lure tour bus groups off I-90 for what Debbie Vorpahl calls "a fun little stop." (In fact, by mid-1998, the town had already entertained eleven tour groups from the Spam-loving state of Hawaii.)

"Everybody's done Disney World and Branson," says Vorpahl. "Group tour operators are always looking for something unique. And no other community in the world can boast they are the capital of Spam luncheon meat."

cuts, a conflict that became the subject of an Oscar-winning documentary film, *American Dream*. For the next year Austin was a town divided. Opponents declared their positions on T-shirts that read "I Love Hormel" or "Cram Your Spam," and just ordering ham and eggs at a restaurant known to serve Hormel products was enough to start a fistfight.

By 1995, however, bitterness over the strike had receded enough for Austin to be able to officially acknowledge the obvious: For better or worse, the town is best known as the home of Spam. In February of that year, by official mayoral declaration, Austin became Spam Town, USA. The moniker now shows up on street banners, postage cancellation stamps, souvenir

Putting SPAM on a Pedestal: An Idea Just Slightly Ahead of Its Time

The Spam Town, USA, tourism campaign is a modest meeting of town and company compared to the idea Austin banker Burt Plehal had in 1965 for a community building that looked like a giant Spam can. Inspired by local hotel owner Dave Averbook's equally offbeat 1964 idea of putting a large pig on a pedestal near I-90, Plehal proposed a Spam building, also visible from the freeway, that would contain a rooftop observation deck, a TV-radio station, business development offices, and a tourist information center.

In his proposal for the building Plehal wrote, "This [pig] idea has merit but it would seem that almost every town along the freeway has hogs, but only Austin has Spam. . . . Why not put Spam on a pedestal?" Plehal commissioned a drawing and pitched his idea to many local community groups until a Hormel executive, upset by mail accusing the company of coming up with a "monstrosity" and "monument to poor taste," asked him to cease and desist.

Fast forward to 1995: Plehal, by now retired, gets a call from another company executive who asks for a copy of the Spam building artist's sketch. It seems Hormel Foods is contemplating using the revenues from its merchandising catalog to create a new Spam museum that would also house the Austin Convention and Visitors Bureau, a theater, and community meeting rooms.

A Spam can building would probably be prohibitively expensive, but Hormel Foods archivist Paulette Cummings says the company has been looking into the idea of putting some kind of Spam can replica on the museum property, including "maybe something people could drive through."

SPAM Goes to War

War changes you. Although this statement is usually made about people, it's also true of Spam luncheon meat. Before being drafted to feed the troops in World War II, Spam was just an innocent new food product advertised with the wide-eyed words "miracle meat in a can." Once enlisted, it was one of the most reviled foodstuffs known to man as well as the none-too-flattering symbol of America to the rest of the world. American GIs called it "ham that didn't pass its physical," "meat loaf without basic training," "the real reason war was hell."

Jay Hormel could not have seen this coming. Still, it almost seemed that way from the vehemence with which he initially opposed U.S. involvement in World War II, cofounding the isolationist America

First Committee and hiring a Broadway composer to write a song that he hoped would popularize his opinion, "This Ain't Our War!":

> *Never interfere if you should hear a battle through your wall,*
> *So your neighbor and his wife may not agree,*
> *And that's the way the U.S.A. should feel about the brawl,*
> *Taking place across the sea.*
> *THIS AIN'T OUR WAR!*

Jay's consciousness was raised about the war (if not about domestic violence) by Pearl Harbor, and it's a good thing because World War II was a bonanza for the Hormel company. Between 1939 and 1942, its net sales doubled to almost $120 million and annual pork processing reached an all-time high of 1.6 million head, mostly because of Uncle Sam. And by 1944, 90 percent of all Hormel canned goods were going to military or military aid programs.

Uncle Sam Wants SPAM!

Canned pork luncheon meat was an early favorite of the armed forces' central food purchasing office in Chicago because it was nutritious, filling, affordable, and shelf-stable. According to a 1946 report, the government bought a lot of it, especially at first, when it was one of only ten canned meats purchased to feed the troops (compared to sixty later). In fact, before the war was over, the army alone had received 150 million pounds.

Although luncheon meat showed up in some portable K ration and parachute bailout packs, it was principally purchased as a B ration to be served in rotation with other meats behind the lines overseas and at camps and bases in the States. But distribution difficulties and wartime emergencies, together with the large initial shipments, resulted in a chorus of GIs who complained about having to eat the stuff once, twice, even three times a day.

"You had it fried in the morning with chemical eggs. They burned it black as a painted door. They'd cut it up and put it into stews. They put it in sandwiches. They

Field Ration K

MAY BE ON <u>YOUR</u> MENU SOME DAY!

"Cheer up, Joe, you never had SPAM for <u>breakfast in bed</u> . . ."

DON'T BLAME YOUR GROCER WHEN HE'S OUT OF SPAM

JACK THOMPSON, Hormel man now with Anti-Aircraft Battery ▆▆▆ in ▆▆▆, writes of the amount of Spam being used by the armed forces: "Because I am far away doesn't mean I am missing Hormel meats. We have Spam quite often here."

baked it with tomato sauce. They gave it to us on the beach. You got so you really hated it," recalls World War II Navy veteran Thomas D. Clancy.

SPAMouflage

Most GI cooks quickly ran out of ideas for fixing Spam. A wartime cartoon shows one talking excitedly to his mess sergeant: "I've got it! Something different! We'll slice Spam lengthwise!" However, a few rose to the challenge, coming up with recipes for Spam meatballs wrapped in fresh jungle vine leaves, Spam à la mode, and Spam chop suey. "Men have been known to get three bites into a second helping before realizing it's the old, familiar enemy," the soldier newspaper *Yank* said of the chop suey. Its cook-creator, one Sergeant Ernest Briscoe, credited his culinary success with Spam to a childhood admiration for Houdini.

The deception was actually deeper than most GIs suspected because the stuff Briscoe and most of the rest of the military chefs were serving was actually not Spam but a generic luncheon meat made from a government recipe and packed in six-pound, olive green, government-issue tin fatigues by Hormel and three other meatpacking companies. Unlike Spam, this luncheon meat contained no ham and was cooked and salted much more in order to withstand both the wintertime cold of Ireland and the tropical heat of the Philippines. But when Hormel tried to explain this to a GI who wrote to ask the company to stop shipping soldiers so much Spam, it suddenly found itself ambushed and under attack.

Under the headline "Spam Really Wasn't Spam," a story in the January 14, 1944, issue of *Yank* began this way: "Pfc. Lewis B. Closser, a GI at Guadalcanal, has made the most startling discovery of the war. He has found that there is not a single can of Spam in the whole U.S. Army."

Yank went on to talk about Closser's complaints to Hormel about Spam and the company's patient explanation of the qualitative difference between six-pound government Spam and the real thing. But

Instead of cake, this Marine stationed in Saipan got a can of K rations, possibly containing Spam, for his twenty-second birthday.

Adversity Verse

This ode to wartime Spam weariness (Spamschmerz) was widely promulgated and credited to many different soldiers as well as to the ever-popular Anonymous.

Ode to SPAM

Now Jackson had his acorns
And Grant his precious rye;
Teddy had his poisoned
    beef—
Worse you couldn't
    buy.
The doughboy had
    his hardtack
Without the
    navy's jam,
But armies on
    their stom-
    achs move—
And this one moves
    on Spam.

For breakfast they will
        fry it;
For supper it is baked;
For dinner it goes delicate—
They have it pat-a-caked.
Next morning it's with flapjacks,
Or maybe powdered eggs—
For God's sake where do they get it?
It must come in by kegs.

Oh, surely for the evening meal
They'll cook up something new!
But the cooks they are uncanny,
Now the Spam is in the stew.
And thus the endless cycle goes;
It never seems to cease—
There's Spam in cake and Spam in pie
        And Spam in rancid grease.

We've had it tucked in salads,
        With cabbage for corned
        beef.
        We've had it for an
        entrée
        And also aperitif.
        We've had it with
        spaghetti,
        With chili and with
        rice.
        (We all remember
        one bright day
        We had it only
        twice.)

        Back home I have an
        angel
        Whose name I want to change.
        I'll purchase her a fancy home
        With a brand-new modern range;
But marital bliss is sure to cease
If I ever ask for ham
And find my eggs are looking up
From a gol-darned slice of Spam.

ultimately *Yank* seemed unimpressed. Borrowing from Shakespeare, the writer concluded: "What's in a name? That which we call Spam by any other name would taste as lousy."

As if that wasn't bad enough, the article triggered a barrage of letters to Hormel, *Yank,* and *Yank*'s overseas counterpart, *Stars and Stripes,* from GIs who swore they had eaten the real Spam and GI cooks

"YANK, THE ARMY WEEKLY"

who swore they had served it. The argument ended when *Yank* published a photograph of a grinning GI popping out from behind a six-foot-tall barricade of real Spam cans and shipping boxes over the caption "We still say it's Spam and we still say to hell with it."

SPAMgate

Going back to its invoices for an explanation, Hormel discovered that in September 1942 the army had bought a substantial order of real Spam as an in-a-pinch substitute for the government kind. At that time, Hormel was also shipping vast quantities of the real

Spam to Allies as part of the government's lend-lease aid program, and some of that could also have ended up in the hands of quartermasters, a beleaguered Jay Hormel explained to a *Stars and Stripes* correspondent assigned to investigate the Spam gaffe. That story was illustrated with a cartoon of a soldier standing in Jay's office with a gun hidden behind his back, echoing a spoof of the World War I–era song "Mademoiselle from Armentieres," then making the soldier rounds:

> *We're saving three shells and*
> *we'll fire them well*
> *At Lewis [of the miners*
> *union], at Congress, and*
> *George A. Hormel . . .*
> *Hinky dinky parlez-vous.*

Not all soldiers attacked Hormel. In fact, one, who said he "used to earn my dough packing Spam, so I should know," defended the company in this widely published poem:

Of course we get a lot
of meat
From loaves
or cans
when'er
we eat,
But every
thing that's
packed in tin
Isn't Spam from Austin,
Minn.

Spam's okay . . .
it's always
swell,

But everything that's packed in tin

And when you taste it you can tell;
So don't shout loudly your complaint
That all loaf meat is Spam . . . it ain't!

SPAMschmerz

Other soldiers thought the Spam flap was as point-less as the debate about the "best" way to be killed in combat. Dead is dead and luncheon meat is lun-cheon meat, especially to someone who has been eat-ing it three times a day for days on end.

Walter P. McClatchey was starving and freezing the snowy winter day an Air Force plane dropped boxes of supplies to his U.S. Army outfit in Belgium. His joy turned to outrage when he saw that the food consisted of several cases of Spam, and so did that of his fellow soldiers. "We shot the hell out of it," McClatchey recalls. He says even the German prisoners wouldn't eat it.

Ex–Army Staff Sergeant Norman Bowman understands why: "They smeared something on it. I think it was motor grease. It was warmed—kind of. . . . They served it with various forms of dehydrated potato, dehydrated milk, dehydrat-ed eggs. . . . Oh, it was stomach-turning gross." But at least Bowman had the advantage of digesting this meal on the ground. According to the war history *Lost Ships of Guadalcanal*, members of the Cactus Air Force at Guadalcanal also had to battle painful intestinal gas pro-duced by Spam in the reduced pressure atmosphere of their airplane cockpits.

isn't Spam from Austin, Minn.

Excerpt from "Talk of the Town," *New Yorker*, August 11, 1945

We had a drink Thursday afternoon with Jay Hormel, the man responsible for Spam, when he happened to be in town. Mr. Hormel . . . is tired of being identified as the man responsible for Spam. He feels sure that he has heard all the Spam gags worth hearing and thousands of Spam gags not worth hearing, and . . . he has the drawn, trapped air of a man who knows he is cer-tain to hear a good many thousands more. In his office at the Hormel plant in Austin, Minnesota, he keeps what he calls his

Scurrilous File, in which he dumps the letters of abuse that are sent to him by soldiers everywhere in the world. "If they think Spam is terrible," Mr. Hormel told us, "they ought to have eaten the bully beef we had in the last war. . . ."

Mr. Hormel toyed with his drink for a moment, then went on. . . . "We didn't even get around to putting Spam on the market until 1937, and before that we'd put up canned ham, chili con carne, soup, chicken and the Dinty Moore line of spaghetti and meatballs. Sometimes I wonder if we shouldn't have . . ." Mr. Hormel didn't finish the sentence. We got the distinct impression that being responsible for Spam might be too great a burden for any one man. "It's all right," he said defensively in a moment. "Damn it, we eat it in our own home." He shook his head and added, "Trouble is, we eat a lot of things in our home that other people won't eat. My wife is French—I married her after the last war—and she likes calves' brains and stuff like that."

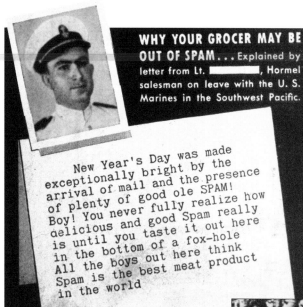

War-era Spam ads put a good face on the Spam overload abroad and the shortages back home.

the European–African–Middle Eastern Campaign Medal for service, the Spam Ribbon. The USO toured the Spam Circuit, food supply depots were Spam Canyons, and a number of U.S. military encampments dubbed themselves Spamville.

Spam also inspired a substantial body of literature during the war—stories, jokes, cartoons, verses, even a prayer. In one of the many cartoons, two stray dogs that feed out of a mess tent garbage can complain about the lack of variety in their diet. Says one to the other, "I'm getting a little tired of Spam, aren't you?" The prayer is a parody of the classic bedtime

Many of the complaints about Spam were similar to those made about bully beef and canned salmon (derisively called goldfish) during World War I. Spam also shared its status as "most hated foodstuff of World War II" with dried chipped beef on toast—better known as SOS (for shit on a shingle)—and an ersatz lemon drink powder that soldiers more commonly used as a hair rinse or stove cleaner.

Still, hatred of lemon powder and SOS never reached the level of institution or art as it did with Spam. Spam was incorporated into the language of the war: Uncle Sam became Uncle Spam. The European invasion fleet was called the Spam Fleet, and

Different Uses for Desperate Men: SPAM as Playing Cards, Gun Grease, and Octopus Bait

Spam was never really dropped from planes to neutralize hostile populations the way some wartime comics suggested. But Allies who ate it—as well as those who couldn't stand to—found many alternative uses for the meat and its can.

World War II veteran Anthony C. Ferri says Spam's fattiness made it perfectly suited for use as a skin conditioner like Vaseline, as a gun lubricant, as a waterproof dressing for leather boots, tents, and matches, and, mixed with lighter fluid or gasoline, as a substitute Sterno. And he

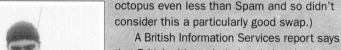

says if he and his GI buddies ever ran out of candles, a twisted piece of cloth inserted into an open can of partially eaten Spam shed almost as much light.

Some Korean War GIs who had no playing cards but plenty of Spam claim to have inked card faces on slices of Spam and played poker with them for three months. "We lost the deuce of diamonds when a dog ate it. But the rest of the deck didn't begin to shred until spring," one private first class participant told newspaper columnist and ex-GI Larry Maddry.

While his ship was at anchor off Omaha Beach, World War II Navy veteran Howard Hovey caught an octopus using just a hand line and Spam for bait. (Hovey likes

octopus even less than Spam and so didn't consider this a particularly good swap.)

A British Information Services report says that British citizens holed up in bomb shelters made more than six thousand toy trains, cars, and animals out of Spam and sardine cans during World War II.

Army mess sergeants in remote locations used soldered, flattened Spam cans to make pots and pans. At least one U.S. fighter pilot told of repairing holes in his aircraft's wings and fuselages with them!

But the best "alternative use" wartime story concerns a certain Corporal Dillon Hopson of the Forty-third Infantry Division.

It seems that Hopson was driving a jeep loaded down with hot food to deliver to some troops when a Japanese soldier, grenade in hand, stepped out from the side of the road. According to an International News Service report, Hopson grabbed fifteen slices of Spam and assorted knives and forks and threw them at the Japanese soldier, causing the grenade to go off before it left his hand. The newspaper report doesn't say whether the Japanese soldier was stopped by the suddenness of Hopson's attack or the thought of possibly having to eat the Spam.

What remained of Spam after the meat, the military used to make pitchers, pots, and pans.

GETTYSBURG
PENNSYLVANIA 17325

June 29, 1966

My dear Tim:

I have just learned from our mutual friend, Jack Cornelius, that your company is celebrating its seventy-fifth anniversary in business.

May I offer you my heartiest congratulations.

You might be surprised to learn that I have long felt a certain kinship with your company.

During World War II, of course, I ate my share of SPAM along with millions of other soldiers. I'll even confess to a few unkind remarks about it -- uttered during the strain of battle, you understand. But as former Commander in Chief, I believe I can still officially forgive you your only sin: sending us so much of it.

Later, as a somewhat inexperienced political candidate, I shared with you the friendship and wise counsel of your advertising agency, BBDO. I must say, I believe they had a tougher job with me than selling SPAM to ex-servicemen. Happily, we all succeeded together.

One more thing we have in common -- our enthusiasm for golf. Were it possible, I would enjoy a round with you very much. But, Tim, I'm afraid you'd have to slow down your whirlwind pace a bit. I have this old "football knee" that nags me, but as a player yourself, I know you understand.

My very best wishes to you and to your company for its continuing success.

Sincerely yours

Dwight D. Eisenhower

Mr. H. H. Corey
Hormel Company
Austin, Minnesota

Spam got a presidential pardon in this letter from former President Dwight D. Eisenhower to retired Hormel President H. H. "Tim" Corey.

rhyme: "Now I lay me down to sleep and pray the Lord the Spam don't keep."

The literature—and the problem—reached the highest ranking officer in the U.S. military. "I ate my share of Spam along with millions of other soldiers," Commander in Chief Dwight D. Eisenhower wrote to a retired Hormel president years later. "I'll even confess to a few unkind remarks about it—uttered during the strain of battle, you understand." But at least he was in a position to do something about it. When the quartermaster's office began developing a new Five-in-One portable kitchen ration,

Eisenhower insisted it contain no Spam because "there is too much Spam now."

SPAM, SPAM, SPAM, SPAM, SPAM

Soldiers stationed in Allied countries where the luncheon meat was being supplied via lend-lease, such as England, couldn't find relief from it even at local restaurants. Said syndicated newspaper columnist Robert Ruark of London during the blitz: "There was no fish and chips and only the black market could find you a piece of gristly meat at a guinea an ounce, but Spam sandwiches were available in every tea shop."

They were also available in all the fine restaurants, according to London-based war correspondent Ralph Morse. "No matter what I order in a restaurant, I always get camouflaged Spam," Morse told *Life* magazine in a war-era letter to

Edward R. Murrow reported on the Brits' gratitude for lend-lease Spam, which showed up in sandwiches on the menu of this ration-era British lunch wagon.

the editor accompanied by close-up table shots of *vol au vent* (French pastry filled with Spam and smothered with sauce), American *schnitzel garni* (Spam mixed in bread crumbs, bound with egg, and fried in oil), *chaudfroid de volaille Yorkaise* (Spam with potato salad and greens), and *Spam réformé* (Spam in Algerian wine sauce with green vegetables).

This kind of experience is undoubtedly the indirect source of Monty Python's famous 1970 Spam skit as well as the reason England became known as Spamland, and American soldiers stationed there, Spams. Edward R. Murrow underscored Spam's omnipresence in the Christmas Eve 1942 broadcast of his CBS radio show, *This Is London:* "Although the Christmas table will not be lavish," he reported, "there will be Spam luncheon meat for everyone."

Murrow's "everyone" included former British Prime Minister Margaret Thatcher, then a teenager working in her family's grocery store. "We had friends in and I can quite vividly remember we opened a tin of Spam luncheon meat," said Thatcher of 1943's Boxing Day, an English holiday observed the day after Christmas. "We had some lettuce and tomatoes and peaches, so it was Spam and salad."

SPAM's Foreign Allies

Ordinary Brits seemed at least as appreciative. When one British newspaper reprinted a *New Yorker* interview with Jay Hormel and others reported on some disparaging remarks an English music hall comic made about burnt Spam, British housewives rushed to the luncheon meat's defense.

Mrs. Amelia A. Garrett of London called Spam "the best tinned food that I've tasted in two wars. . . . It's 100 percent nourishment—and tasty." Mrs. Nesa Beardmore of South Wales wrote to Jay Hormel, "I cannot believe that you have received many letters abusing Spam. We think it is . . . twice blessed—firstly in its fragrant aroma when one opens the tin, and secondly in its perfect flavour and texture." To this day, Doreen Bussey Moseley says champagne and caviar "could never compare" with the "precious, succulent, beautiful Spam" served at her wartime wedding in northern England. But Dorothy Black of Rudgwick outdid them all in a letter to the editor of the May 1945 *Ladies' Home Journal:* "Only those who

have eaten [Spam] at dawn, toasted on the end of a knitting needle at a bomb [shelter], amongst debris, can really know [how good it is]."

Russia was another lend-lease Spam recipient,

Nikita Khrushchev with corn, the food of pigs, the source of Spam—a savior of his army.

Spam Réformé

No SPAM Fritters over the White Cliffs of Dover

Spam may have been a "wartime delicacy" to former British Prime Minister Margaret Thatcher, but the suggestion of Spam fritter competitions as a way to celebrate the fiftieth anniversary of D-Day put a later British administration into a political frying pan in 1994. Veterans organizations and the opposition Labour Party attacked the plan as being far too frivolous a way to commemorate an end-of-the-war military operation that left thirty-seven thousand Allied dead. The uproar reached a crescendo when Dame Vera Lynn, a singer famous for her rendition of "There'll Be Bluebirds over the White Cliffs of Dover," said she wouldn't take part in any celebration veterans didn't want. Prime Minister John Major backed down and June 6, 1994, came and went with no word on who makes the best Spam fritters in England.

Singer Vera Lynn didn't want to fritter away the goodwill she created with British fighting men 'round the piano by fighting their opinion of proposed D-Day commemorative Spam fritter cooking contests.

and although Russian soldiers also joked about it, leader Nikita Khrushchev was grateful. As he wrote in his biography, *Khrushchev Remembers,* "We had lost our most fertile, food-bearing lands—the Ukraine and the Northern Caucasus. Without Spam we wouldn't have been able to feed our army."

SPAM: Still on the Home Front Range

Meanwhile, back in the United States, there was a tin shortage and a ban on the domestic sale of most of the brand-name canned products Hormel made before the war—except Spam. "No bone, no waste, no surplus fat—full value for your points when you spend your stamps for Spam," advertisements intoned to ration-book-wielding housewives. Spam's convenience was also stressed in an ad featuring two Rosie the Riveters.

ROSIE 1: What do you cook at home for Dick?

ROSIE 2: Spam—it's good and easy and quick.

The corners of most of the wartime ads for Spam were taken over by thumbnail photos of

A Mess of Ways to Serve SPAM

No World War II–era military cook would think of stepping under a mess tent without an arsenal of Spam recipes. Retired U.S. Army Master Sergeant Joseph Gregoria was no exception. Gregoria acquired these nameless recipes (here adapted for use with standard store-size cans) from the Army, his own imagination, and a gourmet chef hired to teach mess sergeants how to make the dreaded luncheon meat delicious.

Cut one can Spam into cubes. Add one can creamed corn. Add enough flour to make thick doughlike mixture. Fry in deep fat until brown. Serve hot with mustard or horseradish sauce.

. . . . .

Cut one can Spam into long strips. Dip in 2 cups pancake batter. Deep fry in fat until brown. Serve with mustard, tomato, or horseradish sauce.

. . . . .

Cut one can Spam into thin pieces. Dip in an egg batter made of one egg and 1/2 cup milk. Roll in crushed cornflakes. Fry in deep fat for 3 to 4 minutes. Serve with spicy tomato sauce.

. . . . .

Cut one can Spam into cubes. Fry in open pan until brown. Discard juice. Add to 2 gallons of potato soup.

. . . . .

Chop one can Spam very fine. Add to six medium cooked, mashed potatoes. Form into balls. Fry in deep fat.

. . . . .

Cube one can Spam. Fry in open pan until golden brown and fairly crisp. Drain well. Add to macaroni or potato salad.

. . . . .

Slice one can Spam. Brown Spam on both sides. Top each slice with a fried egg, sunny-side up. Serve with Hollandaise sauce.

. . . . .

Asked why so many of his preparations involved frying, Gregoria said, "Trying to bake on those diesel stoves was impossible. You had no control." And as for seasoning, he said, "I never added salt to any of the recipes because Spam was salty enough."

Hormel employees-turned-soldiers commenting on their experiences with Hormel products abroad. Corporal Harley McGuiness had this to say at the bottom of an ad featuring a recipe for Spam birds, stuffing-filled Spam slices speared with toothpicks that looked like wings: "No matter what part of the world you go to, Hormel products are in all out use to fill the boys up and they really are treats to eat."

Another ad featured the words of an unidentified Hormel-salesman-turned-U.S.-Marine, who said: "New Year's Day was made exceptionally bright by the arrival of mail and the presence of plenty of good ole Spam! Boy! You never fully realize how delicious and good Spam really is until you taste it out here in the bottom of a fox-hole. All the boys out here think Spam is the best meat product in the world."

Wartime PropaSPAMda?

These testimonials seemed to contradict what Hormel was telling soldiers about the difference between Spam and the government luncheon meat they were

eating. Although published in Stateside magazines such as *Time* and intended for civilian consumption, the ads inevitably reached GIs. And to borrow the language and tone of the Marine from Hormel: Boy! Were they ever mad!

One soldier sent Hormel a modified copy of the Spam birds ad with *stuff* in the word *stuffing* underlined and the words *up your ass* added. And among those who wrote to chide Hormel for insulting their intelligence in the "good ole Spam" ad were six Marines stationed in San Francisco. "You know as well or better than we do that Spam is a mighty unpopular food in the Armed Forces. . . . Unlike the cracks against Brooklyn . . . those against Spam . . . are well deserved." The Marines applauded the decision to delete the soldier's name from the ad, but not for the national security reasons that motivated Hormel. "I am afraid the Lieutenant would be lynched by his boys, or turned over to the Japs, if his name did appear," one of them wrote.

Miracle Meat Market

As if the soldiers didn't get enough luncheon meat in their rations, some, incredibly, received cans of the real thing in the mail from home. One of the most dramatic cartoons to address the situation showed a GI hanging high above a kicked-away stool with an opened package containing cans of Spam.

Enterprising GIs would trade such unwanted gifts for rum or cigarettes. British and Canadian soldiers looked with envy on the Americans' "vast quantities of tinned meats, fruits and vegetables," in the words of one officer, and so were prime trading candidates. In some countries, a can of Spam could also be bartered for manual labor, intelligence, even the services of a prostitute.

Marguerite Patten, an English cookbook writer who developed recipes for the British government's Ministry of Food during the war, says bringing a can to the home of a British date was like bringing a joint of beef would be today (thus, perhaps, explaining the origins of the terms *pickup joint* and *meat market*?).

Some civilians even risked imprisonment to get Spam. They included participants in a Neapolitan black market for Spam reported on in the winter 1995 issue of *Granta* magazine. Writer Norman Lewis, a soldier in World War II, recalled visiting one restaurant that charged twice as much for Spam as for anything else on the menu. Asked why, the owner oscillated his hips and said, "Per fare amore." In Naples, at that time, Spam was considered an aphrodisiac!

SPAMbrosia

But no one appreciated Spam as much as the refugees who received it as part of relief efforts or during reoccupation. John Dunmore got his first taste of Spam as part of Red Cross food relief packages delivered to the German-occupied Channel

Islands only months before food stocks were scheduled to run out. "It was a luxury," he recalls. "People washed out the tin carefully after use because the water one rinsed it out with made soup—thin, but precious."

Irena Urdang de Tour calls the CARE packages of Spam, chocolate, and soup she received in the ruins of Warsaw after years of slave labor in Berlin "ambrosia": "They were the answer to an SOS, like Robinson Crusoe, a blood transfusion, salvation—I could go on forever."

Of course these were desperate, starving people. American soldiers, by contrast, ate more Spam than they had as civilians. In fact, they ate so much that Jay Hormel worried that Spam might become a wartime casualty.

Foreign Service

PUBLISHED MONTHLY BY THE VETERANS OF FOREIGN WARS OF THE UNITED STATES

November 1947

Hormel's worst fears. The book *Mr. Whitekeys' Alaska Bizarre* tells the story of a Spam-weary returned veteran in a bar who paused from his war stories long enough to ask the stranger he was talking to what he had done during the war. "I had a national priority defense job at the Spam factory," the man said, just seconds before the vet landed his first punch. It took everyone in the bar to pull the two men apart.

One veteran's son who phoned in to a Wisconsin radio discussion program recalled how Spam was served in his household only when his parents were fighting. His father had been in the army and "really detested Spam," he said, so his mother fixed it whenever she wanted to punish him.

In 1946 Jay Hormel decided to take the offensive by hiring ex-GI women to travel the country and promote Spam and other Hormel products. But Spam sales went up even before the Hormel Girls hit the road. For every soldier who swore he would never eat Spam again and stuck to it, there seemed to be two who became Spam customers as a result of being introduced to it during

Victory over SPAM?

When *Stars and Stripes* asked random GIs what they would do if their girlfriends served them Spam on their first night at home, the answers only confirmed

the war. Popular culture mavens Jane and Michael Stern attribute Spam's postwar popularity to the Helsinki syndrome, that condition in which captive people come to feel affection for their captors.

In recent years Hormel has gone beyond saying that Spam survived the war and thrived in sales to suggesting that Spam saved lives and helped win the war. A contrarian view is expressed in an *Adam* cartoon strip in which the title character delivers a Spam sandwich lunch along with a lecture about how Normandy, Iwo Jima, and Okinawa were all fueled by Spam. "Sadly, for many brave young servicemen, Spam was the last thing they ever tasted," Adam solemnly tells his wife. "Has anyone looked into that coincidence?" is her reply.

Spam also saw action in Korea, although much less often than in World War II, and by Vietnam canned meats had been largely replaced by less bulky, lighter weight foods.

U.S. troops in 1990's Persian Gulf War, partly out of deference to the Islamic ban on pork. However, cans of the real Spam were brisk sellers at portable PXs set up during Desert Storm, as they are in U.S. military commissaries around the world. Veterans who overloaded on Spam during World War II or in Korea may be amused to hear the explanation offered by Gene Hopkins, manager of government sales and marketing for Hormel Foods: "Soldiers like it because it's a change of pace from what they usually eat."

Meating the Needs of Today's Military

Although "luncheon meat, canned" is still served to GIs, it's a discretionary part of today's garrison rations and it's used only occasionally.

"We've come a long way from Spam," said Colonel Eldon Askew, the retired director of military nutrition research at the U.S. Army Research Institute of Environmental Medicine in Natick, Massachusetts, in a July 1994 *New York Times* article about the new, nutritionally correct military food.

In fact, no luncheon meat at all was served to

Making SPAM

Very few large American companies still give public plant tours, and Hormel Foods is no exception. Fear of lawsuits and industrial espionage is the primary reason. It's a shame for public understanding of our industrial culture in general and of Spam in particular, for public tours would quickly slaughter all the unfounded rumors about the nasty things Spam luncheon meat contains.

The floors in the Austin, Minnesota, plant of Hormel Foods glisten with water from frequent washings. There's no blood and no smell. From certain vantage points, at least, the plant looks more like an electronics factory than a packinghouse, and, truth to tell, a can of Spam lasts longer than many televisions and fax machines made these days. The Austin plant

is one of two U.S. locations where Spam is produced. The other is in Fremont, Nebraska, where all seven-ounce cans are made as well as 65 percent of the twelve ouncers.

Twelve-ounce Spam is one of about four hundred products created by Hormel Foods in its flagship plant in Austin, a low, sleek brick building big enough to accommodate twenty-three professional football games at a November-like forty degrees. The activity that actually goes on here is less violent than football but no less frenetic. Touring the finishing areas for sausage, bacon, and hot dogs is like walking through a movie set that is constantly changing. If you were not careful, you could easily get struck down by a forklift filled with pork chops or caught in the back of the neck by a string of swinging hot dogs. That's why everyone wears a hard hat.

The Spam area seems calm and orderly by comparison. That's probably because it is and long has been the plant's most mechanized. In fact, over the years the main change has been in the increasing sophistication of the machinery and in a corresponding decline in the number of people needed to operate it. Today fewer than thirteen people keep the Spam line moving at a rate of about 435 cans a minute. As one twenty-five-year veteran of the Spam department in Fremont puts it, "The work isn't hard. Mainly what we do is watch."

What workers mainly watch are dials and Spam cans. Although

Meat, the early years

Sausage   Hot Dogs
Spam   Bologna

What's in There?

Perfectly rectangular, pansy pink, soft and mushy, Spam is like nothing found in nature. No wonder people are nervous about its ingredients—a nervousness that comes out in joking speculation that it contains "everything but the squeal."

The truth is that by modern-day packaged food standards, Spam has a very short, and not at all scary, ingredients list:

PORK WITH HAM. These are the primary ingredients. From 85 to 95 percent of Spam is pork from a pig's shoulders. The remaining 5 to 15 percent is trimmings from the pig's rear end, which is more commonly and appetizingly known as ham. (Interestingly and confusingly enough, one of the two pieces of a pig shoulder is called the butt, even though it is nowhere near the animal's rear end.) The ratio of pork to ham varies with ham prices. By U.S. Department of Agriculture definition, luncheon meat may not contain nonmeat fillers. It also must be free of pig snouts, lips, and ears. Although it may contain pig tongues and hearts, these parts must be listed separately on the label if it does. They're blessedly absent from Spam's.

SALT. In addition to providing flavor and firmness, this second ingredient acts as a preservative. Spam would have to be cooked longer if not for the salt. Up until the early '70s, Spam also contained pepper in the form of the easily blendable pepper cream. However, it was decided that the pepper really didn't add much flavor.

WATER. Government regulations limit the amount of water that can be added to luncheon meat to 3 percent of the product's total weight, but a little is necessary to blend the other ingredients with the meat.

SUGAR. This is there solely for flavor.

SODIUM NITRITE. This final ingredient acts primarily as a preservative: It inhibits the bacterial growth that can cause botulism. Although some studies have linked nitrites to cancer, the government has deemed the risk of death from botulism to be so much greater than the risk nitrites pose for cancer that it approves their use. Sodium nitrite adds to the flavor of Spam, too, and it also gives it its perky pink color. Without it, Spam would look as brown as any other cooked meat.

Spam starts with pigs, pig slaughtering has never taken place in the Spam area and hasn't been part of Hormel company operations in Austin since the late 1980s. The reason has more to do with the bottom line than with squeamishness. There's a lot less money in butchering animals than in transforming the resulting raw meat into packaged food products. So Hormel now leases out its slaughterhouse in Austin to a company called Quality Pork.

Members of the hog kill gang at the Hormel plant in Austin, Minnesota, were featured in *Fortune* magazine in 1937.

The Pig Squeeze

Spam first comes into the Hormel Foods factory in the form of hog pieces: specifically, pork shoulder—also called picnic meat—and ham. The picnics are so bony that in Spam's early days they had to be carved by hand, but today they are put through a powerful molded hydraulic press that literally squeezes all the meat off. After that, the meat is stored in gondolas that look like huge industrial laundry baskets.

The ham in Spam is still processed by hand. As the workers in the ham line trim hams, they sort the pieces destined for Spam into gondolas marked "white" (for the fattiest pieces) and "red" (for the meatiest).

When it's time to make Spam, the meat-filled gondolas are wheeled from a large refrigerated storage area onto the main floor. The meat is first transferred to one of several cranelike machines and then dumped into an enormous metal trough lined with a big drill bit. There it is ground,

In years gone by, the ingredients for Spam were shoveled by hand into grinding machines.

The Lowdown on the Slippery Stuff

Even people who can get past their fears about what's in Spam often have a problem with the clear, gelatinous material that comes with it and gives it a distinctive "glug, glug" sound when you shake the can.

What *is* that stuff? In a word, gelatin. Like Jell-O, Spam gel is basically the glutinous material that comes from cooking animal tissue. Unlike Jell-O, Spam's gelatin is an unbidden and, for the most part, unwanted by-product of cooking Spam in the can—and not, as many assume, an ingredient added to help slide it out.

Think back to the last time you cooked a roast. In your mind's eye, return to the bottom of the pan you cooked it in. You see a considerable amount of juice mixed in with little scraps of meat and fat, right? If you had put the pan in the refrigerator, the juice and fat would have congealed into gelatin similar to what you find in Spam.

Although cooks acknowledge the common heritage of Spam gel and meat stock and gravy, most hesitate to use the gel in Spam dishes. The Spamettes of Austin, Minnesota, sing of this hesitation in one verse of their Spam spoof of "God Rest Ye Merry Gentlemen":

The only real challenge cooking Spam we now will tell,
Is whether, when we cook it, we should ever use the gel.
Whenever we suggest it we are told to go and think,
Should we use it or pour it down the sink, down the sink?
Should we only use the part of Spam that's pink?

Retired Hormel production manager Helmer Peterson has an answer to the "Should we use it?" question—an unqualified yes. He says Spam gelatin is almost 100 percent protein, extremely nutritious—maybe even the best thing in the can. And indeed, Knox unflavored gelatin, which is similar to the gelatin in a Spam can, has six grams of protein and no fat compared to one gram of protein and two grams of fat in Spam meat of the same weight.

Incidentally, the slippery part of Spam is only the tip of the hog's tail when it comes to gelatin from Hormel Foods. Pig skins passing through the company's plants go on to new life as gelatin pills, gelatin desserts, yogurt, gummy candies, film coatings, shampoos, and skin care products.

---

weighed (the initial batch is eight thousand pounds), and passed under a metal detector to catch the stray knife blade or piece of machinery. A small sample is also analyzed by X ray to ensure a Spam-precise blend of meat and fat.

Stirring Up Some SPAM

The ground meat is then distributed by more gondolas into several vacuum mixers. When open, these mixers look like giant gas grills, but they actually have a refrigerated ammonia outer core that brings the temperature of the meat down to well below

freezing. Then the other things on the Spam ingredients list—salt, water, sugar, and sodium nitrite—are added, the lid is shut to create an airtight seal, and the mixing begins.

The vacuum, cold, and salt all help minimize the amount of juice released by the meat when it is cooked. Without them, a can of Spam would contain much more gelatin.

Troop SPAM

As the meat is being mixed at one end of the Spam production area, machines on the other side of the room are pushing empty, inverted Spam cans off storage pallets one layer at a time. When these marching tin soldiers meet the single-file conveyor line, they become Spam can trains.

Meanwhile 990 pounds of Spam has been manually unloaded from the first mixer, dumped into receivers, and fed through pipes until it reaches cone-shaped can fillers. As the cans travel underneath the fillers, a device picks each one up and deposits the Spam mixture into it in one jerky motion. The can is filled while being lifted to prevent spills and to help maintain the vacuum that was created in the mixer. It's also filled upside down, which is why the top of the Spam loaf is always more squared off than the bottom. (Check it out the next time you open a can.)

At this point, the stuff in the cans looks more like pinkish white clay than Spam. The next step in processing banishes the sight of it with lids, which are affixed and sealed at one of six closing machines. Then the cans are stamped with an identifying code

The huge hydrostatic Spam cooker under construction in 1979.

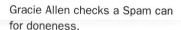

Gracie Allen checks a Spam can for doneness.

and sent on a journey to a six-story-high hydrostatic Spam cooker—a device so big and important to Hormel Foods that the whole Austin plant was built around it.

Meating the Heat

The cooker is called hydrostatic because water is the source of heat and the force behind almost everything else the machine does. As the Spam cans approach the cooker in a line, an arm swings out and pushes twenty-four of them onto a shelf, and then the shelf starts moving upward, like a carnival Ferris wheel. During the next two hours, sixty-six thousand Spam cans will travel up and down eleven chambers in the cooker, and along the way they will be heated to the point of sterilization, washed, and cooled.

By now you've probably surmised something that surprises people unfamiliar with canning: Spam is cooked in its can.

Averting SPAMdamonium

An alarm on the cooker warns its operator of problems. Should any develop, he or she can stop the machine for up to five minutes without compromis-

The Key to an Age-Old Problem: Opening the SPAM Can

The Spam can's unusual oblong shape was designed to increase heat penetration during cooking and to make the luncheon meat fit on square slices of bread. One unwelcome consequence of this shape, though, is that a Spam can is almost impossible to open with an ordinary can opener.

Hence, the Spam key. Surely you old-timers remember the fun of breaking it off the can top, inserting its slot into the metal tab, and winding it around the can until it acquired a metal spiral. That's when you did it right. If you let that little key get off its track, only a hacksaw would get you lunch.

Spam keys were prized by kids not only because they were good at pretend-opening dollhouses and cars but also because they were dangerous. Race car driver Kyle Petty remembers just how dangerous they were. As the designated Spam can opener in his family while growing up, Petty had plenty of experience turning Spam keys. But every single time he opened a Spam can, his mother cautioned him, "Be careful, you'll cut your finger." And no wonder—even

adults cut themselves using those keys. By all rights early Spam cans should have carried a warning—"Opening may be hazardous to your health"—or at least been accompanied by a Band-Aid.

Long aware of these problems, Hormel in 1967 came out with what com-

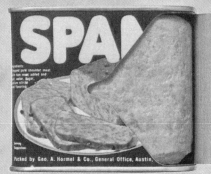

pany promotional literature described as "an entirely new marvel in convenience packaging of Spam." The RingSide, or side-opening, Spam can featured a ring pull tab that consumers lifted up and pulled until most of one side of the can was in their hand, with the Spam brick largely exposed. Hormel sprang for Spam's very first television commercial

to show how the "new marvel" worked.

Nine out of ten housewives surveyed by a research firm hired by Hormel said they preferred the new aluminum can to the old one. But consumers did not like the higher cost. And Hormel did not like the way the perforations would sometimes open during shipping. Moreover, the side panel sometimes broke off or curled as the consumer pulled the tab, and the potential for injury was even greater than with the old key. So, after only about a year and a half, the key returned.

The company introduced the top pull tab in 1989. Spam then opened like a soda can except that the tab—the whole top of the can—was a lot bigger and thicker and therefore harder to pull off. To answer people's complaints about that, Hormel Foods introduced an ergonomically improved corner pull tab on a classy-looking gold-hued can in 1998—the same year the company began selling necklaces featuring sterling silver replicas of the old Spam key.

SAVE IT! No more keys for duration. Or use can opener

ing the quality of the cooked meat. The Spam crew has only three minutes to solve any problems with the packing equipment that receives the cans after cooking. This stay of execution comes via an over-

head circular conveyor-to-nowhere that is sort of the Spam factory equivalent of an airplane holding pattern. When three minutes is not long enough, the Spam line resembles the classic *I Love Lucy* chocolate factory episode, as some workers scramble to put the cans in cardboard tote bins

Hormel pulls it off...

The Faces (and Typefaces) of SPAM

With the switch to polypropylene labels in 1997, the classic Spam loaf image on the Spam can was replaced by a Spamburger. Up until then, changes in the design of the can had been modest: In the 1950s, the image of the Spam loaf was flopped, cloves entered the picture, and the tubular lettering ballooned up to near cartoonish proportions. In 1987, Spam got a typeface-lift for its fiftieth birthday, and the letters now sport serifs.

while others try to fix the equipment.

For sixty years Spam cans had lithographed labels and marched around the production floor dressed in their characteristic blue and yellow. But in 1997, to save money and make it easier to change on-can recipes and promotions, Hormel Foods switched to a plain metal can covered with a plastic polypropylene label. The labels come in long rolls that sit at the exit of the hydrostatic cooker. As the cans emerge, a machine puts the film around each one and cuts the label.

If all this goes right, twenty-four freshly labeled cans are fed onto flat pieces of cardboard that are literally formed into boxes around them. When there are enough boxes to fill a pallet, they are shrink-wrapped together before being stamped

with a date and other identifying numbers. A giant robot crane, controlled by a computer, then comes over to transfer the pallet to the racks of shelving that tower over one side of the Spam operation. The same computer-driven crane goes back to fetch the pallets to fill Spam orders. It's only when the pallets reach the loading dock that a human-operated fork-lift takes over.

No Spam can leaves the building until it is at least ten days old. That's because of U.S. Department of Agriculture regulations requiring that one of every

The Spam packaging and storage area of Hormel Foods' Austin, Minnesota, plant, which can accommodate more than twenty million cans of the luncheon meat.

How to Read a SPAM Can

For tracking purposes, in case of problems, the U.S. Department of Agriculture (USDA) requires every can of luncheon meat to be marked with an identifying code. It's stamped on the bottom of a Spam can and looks something like this:

A11068 4
EST. 199 18:19 RS

In the first line, the *A* stands for the Austin, Minnesota, plant of Hormel Foods. If your can has an *F,* it was produced in Fremont, Nebraska, the only other plant that makes Spam. The five numbers after that, *11068,* stand for the date: the eleventh month, sixth day, of 1998. The last number, *4,* identifies the batch the can belongs to. The company changes this number code every two and a half hours or so—about the length of time it takes to produce a can of Spam. A *1* would indicate a can that was part of the day's first batch; a *7,* part of the day's last. Our hypothetical can was made in the middle of Spam's fifteen- to seventeen-hour production day.

As for the second line, *EST. 199* is the establishment number the USDA has given to the Austin plant. If your Spam was made in Fremont, it would read *EST. 199N.* The *18:19* stands for the moment the Spam can was stamped, expressed in twenty-four-hour, or military, time. Our hypothetical can was marching off to be cooked at 6:19 P.M. Finally, *RS* identifies the variety of Spam inside, in this case regular Spam. Cans with *LS* or *SM* contain Spam Lite or Spam Smoke Flavored, respectively.

thousand cans produced be subjected to 100-degree heat to see if it bulges or shows any other signs of being uncooked or unsafe. If there are no problems after ten days, the rest of the batch can begin to be sold.

To head off other problems, Hormel Foods subjects Spam to frequent quality checks. Every Friday morning, for example, all the company executives involved with Spam production meet to open, visually inspect, and taste the Spam from various batches. Taste? Cold, out-of-can Spam at 10:30 A.M.? Pressed on the point, Gary Ray, executive vice president of operations for Hormel Foods, admits that the test is "mostly observation."

Hormel Foods President Joel Johnson holds the five-billionth can of Spam.

SPAMper's Index

Age in years of oldest can of Spam known to have been safely consumed: 25
Recommended shelf life of canned meats for maximum enjoyment, in years: 2
Number of U.S. packing plants that produced Spam in 1986: 3
Number of U.S. packing plants producing Spam today: 2
Number of cans of Spam produced by Hormel Foods' Austin, Minnesota, plant per minute: 435
Number of cans of Spam that can be stored in Hormel Foods' Austin plant: 20,736,000
Year the first can of Spam was produced: 1937
Year the one-billionth can of Spam was produced: 1959
Year the two-billionth can of Spam was produced: 1970
Year the three-billionth can of Spam was produced: 1980
Year the four-billionth can of Spam was produced: 1986
Year the five-billionth can of Spam was produced: 1994
Number of times five billion cans of Spam, placed end to end, would circle the globe: 12.5
Number of years a family of four would have to live to eat five billion cans of Spam at a rate of three cans per day (to the nearest hundredth): 4,563,084.65
Number of foreign countries in which Spam is produced: 4*
Number of cans of Spam produced in foreign countries per year: 30 million
Number of countries in which Spam is still opened with a key: 2**
Year Spam was awarded a prize by the Minnesota Association of Commerce and Industry for being the most "state of the art" Minnesota-manufactured product: 1986

*They are Japan, Korea, the Philippines, and Denmark.
**They are Japan and the Philippines.

1,000,000,000 cans of SPAM

Hat can't contain head swollen with porcine pride.

Pink-tinted outlook on life.

Fanatical grin.

Great taste in accessories.

Purchases given to flights of Spam fancy.

SPAM Fans

Spam luncheon meat is sold in virtually every grocery store in America. In 1997, some sixty-eight million pounds, or ninety million cans, of Spam were purchased in the United States. In volume sales, Spam is the 120th best-selling product out of the thirty thousand sold in the average American supermarket. Despite the jokes, despite the shame—which Hormel once addressed with a button reading, "Join Spam Anonymous: Over 75 million members"—America is home to many, many Spam fans.

People are particularly Spam-crazy in the Southeast, the Southwest, and the noncontiguous states. To be specific, the good folks of Texas, Arkansas, the Virginias, the Carolinas, Mississippi, Alabama, and Alaska eat an average of one can per person per year, or about twice the national average, and those in Hawaii consume even more.

Club SPAM

Alaska's place on the Spam list can probably be attributed largely to the proprietor and piano player of the Fly By Night Club in suburban Anchorage, who goes by the name of Mr. Whitekeys. Featuring a Spam menu, Spam decor, and Spam show numbers, the Fly By Night is a mecca for serious Spam fans. Why and how it achieved that status is almost as mysterious as the bearded, bespectacled Mr. Whitekeys himself.

Whitekeys opened the Fly By Night in 1980 in

Should You Find Yourself in Alaska

Mr. Whitekeys' Fly By Night Club is located at 3300 Spenard Road in suburban Anchorage, Alaska, and is open Tuesdays through Saturdays, 4 P.M. to 1 A.M., from April through December. The main attractions of both restaurant and bar are a Spam menu and a multimedia musical comedy revue about Alaskan culture (including Spam) that changes with the seasons. The show begins at 8:15 P.M. and ends about 10:30 nightly. No smoking on Tuesdays and Thursdays. The cover charge is $12, $15, or $17 depending on the seats. Reservations are required

at least a week in advance. The phone number is 907-279-SPAM.

Mr. Whitekeys is always looking for pictures of Spam in exotic or unusual locations. As his brochure "How to Take Spam Pictures Good" explains, he prefers slides in a horizontal format because they fit the shape of the club's screen. Club patrons whose photos end up being used get a free Spam dish or, if the photo is mentioned in a song, two free tickets to the show. Send photos to the Fly By Night Club at the street address given above (zip code 99503) or drop them by in person during regular club hours.

a location formerly known as the Idle Hour, the Lakeshore Club, VFW Post 1685, the Fancy Moose, the Oar House, the Red Baron, the Flying Machine Mexican Restaurant, and the Co-Pilot Club—the last three names as well as Fly By Night inspired by the airplane tail that makes the club's entrance look like the scene of a recent air disaster. "Going out of Business Regularly in the Same Location for Over Thirty Years" is, in fact, one club advertising slogan.

A few months after opening, the Fly By Night added Spam to its menu and was thereafter required to upgrade from a provisional to a full-fee health permit. The local health inspector explained why: The club was now serving "a hazardous substance." Today the Fly By Night boasts of being the "Home of Spam, Booze, Rhythm & Blues," and its menu of "Gormay Kweezeen" features Spam nachos, Spam potato skins, Spam bagel Dijonnaise, Spamadillas, coconut beer-batter Spam, and Spamburger hamburgers (quadrideckers of Spam, hamburger, bacon, and cheese that make the official Spamburger of Spam, cheese, lettuce, and tomato seem almost like health food). Spam dishes are half off with any bottle

S P A M : A Biography

SPAMtastic
Mincemeat Truffles

These chocolate-covered mincemeat and Spam candies invented by Wanda Larson won first place in the Best Spam Recipe Contest of the 1994 Alaska State Fair and once graced the dessert menu of Mr. Whitekeys' Fly By Night Club in Anchorage.

1 envelope gelatin
2 tablespoons water
1 (12-ounce) can Spam Lite luncheon meat
1 (9-ounce) box condensed mincemeat
1 cup Coffee-mate powdered coffee creamer,
    hazelnut flavor
2 cups flaked coconut
$1/2$ cup black rum
1 teaspoon rum flavoring
1 teaspoon vanilla extract
2 pounds powdered sugar
1 cup walnut pieces
1 24-ounce package semisweet chocolate chips
1 12-ounce package white chocolate chips

Dissolve gelatin in water in microwave about $1^1/2$ minutes. In food processor combine Spam and gelatin for 2 minutes at medium speed. Add mincemeat and coffee creamer. Process 3 minutes at medium speed.

Place Spam mixture in large bowl. Add coconut, rum, rum flavoring, vanilla, and powdered sugar. Mix well. Refrigerate overnight.

Using the large end of a melon baller, form candy into balls with a walnut piece in the center of each one. Freeze candy for several hours.

Melt dark chocolate chips in small bowl in microwave about 5 minutes. Using a two-tined fork, dip each candy ball into dark chocolate, shake off excess, and place on waxed paper.

Melt white chocolate chips in microwave about 3 minutes. Place melted white chips in a Ziploc bag. Snip off a tiny bit of plastic from one corner of bag. Drizzle white chocolate back and forth across candy balls. Allow chocolate to harden. Keep refrigerated up to 10 days. Yields 100 truffles.

of champagne—and free with Dom Perignon. Or get your Frequent Spammer Card punched ten times and have any Spam dish free.

Whitekeys also collects snapshots of Spam cans in famous or exotic locales. Club visitors have obliged by bringing him pictures taken underwater, on top of Mount McKinley, at the Egyptian pyramids, in a maternity room, at the Eiffel Tower, on top of the Great Wall of China, and in front of the Taj Mahal and the Statue of Liberty. Dozens of these photos—some featuring strippers, others poisonous snakes—decorate the walls of the club along with cans of foreign and vintage Spam, cans of Spam's competitors, and a work of art created by running a ten-ton steamroller over two bottles of white-out, a loaf of Spam, and an eight-by-ten glossy photograph of Barry Manilow.

Whitekeys converts some of the photos to slides and sets them to music for the Spam song that is part of the Fly By Night's show, a multimedia musical comedy revue featuring pianist

An exotic dancer who goes by the name of Pillow struts her Spam in Alaska.

Whitekeys and a band known as the Spamtones. Past numbers have included "Spammin' U.S.A.," "Spammin' in the Streets," and "The Ten Commandments of Spam." Some Fly By Night slide shows have also featured photos from the Seattle Spam Carving Contest, the Alaska State Fair Spam recipe contest, and other Alaskan Spam occurrences.

SPAM's Great Alaskan Adventures

In Alaska, snowmobilers breaking trail for the Iditarod have prepared dinner by wiring a can of Spam to their exhaust manifolds. Spam also helped fuel Vernon Tejas's successful February 1988 quest to make the first-ever solo winter climb to the summit of Denali, the highest peak in North America. And according to the 1996 TV movie *Trial at Fortitude Bay*, Inuit Eskimos carry Spam on hunting trips—

A Spam-packing Eskimo.

not to eat, but as protection against out-of-sorts polar bears. Should an unfortunate Eskimo find himself confronted by such a bear, he grabs a can of Spam, slashes it open with his knife, throws it at the bear, and escapes while the bear eats.

Something like this actually happened to Alaskan actress Tracey Williams while she was on a hike one July morning in 1987. Williams thought she was making her own lunch when she opened a can of Spam, put it in a plastic bag, and stashed it in her backpack before setting out. But when a grizzly appeared and knocked her over, she was very glad he preferred the smell of Spam to her.

SPAM Paradise

Spam is even bigger in Hawaii than it is in Alaska. Although the Hawaiian tourist bureau prefers to push its Kona coffee, papayas, pineapples, macadamia nuts, and poi, Spam is what the native people really eat. In fact, Hawaii's annual per capita con-  sumption of four cans, or three pounds, makes it the Spam-eatingest state in the nation. Moreover, Spam's hometown of Austin, Minnesota, has become a standard stop for Hawaiian tour groups visiting the U.S. mainland. Spam is also touted by one of Hawaii's U.S. senators and one of its most celebrated chefs.

Senator Daniel Inouye calls Spam "a delicacy," insisting that the stuff fellow soldiers complained about during World War II was not Spam but pressed

Sam Choy

pork. For Hawaiian TV cooking show star and cookbook author Sam Choy, Spam is an integral part of the menu of island soul food featured at his chain of restaurants. As Choy told a reporter for the *Wall Street Journal*, "The food of the 1990s is all the same—salsa this, balsamic vinegar that. We can offer something totally more exciting."

Spam's power over Hawaiians even supersedes local superstition. It's normally considered bad luck to carry pork on Oahu's mountainous Pali Highway. But truck drivers carrying Spam take that route, and so far no trouble has been reported. "I think it has something to do with the integrity of the container. The can keeps all that wonderful pork sealed up nice and tight and deflects bad luck," local food broker Hoagy Gamble says.

SPAM Musubi—Ono!

Hawaiians' favorite way to eat Spam is in sushi. Consisting of a lightly fried slab of Spam and a Japanese-style ball or cake of rice wrapped together with a belt of seaweed, the so-

Frying Pan Poetry

Award-winning Honolulu poet Lois-Ann Yamanaka offers a taste of island family life in "The Brain" from her collection *Saturday Night at the Pahala Theatre*.

*I get one
splitting
headache.
No ask me questions.
And no move.
First one
who breathe
going get
one good whack
with the fly swatter.
You. Cook the rice.
You. Fry some Spam.
Open one can corn.
Everybody
shut up.
I work all day long,
I come home
and all you doing
is watching tv.
Sit down.
Shut up.
I gotta rest.*

Incidentally, Yamanaka's novel *Wild Meat and the Bully Burgers* also features a dog named Spam.

called Spam omusubi (meaning "rice ball")—or, as it is more commonly known, Spam musubi (MOO-sue-bee)—is as ubiquitous in convenience stores and take-out joints in Hawaii as hot dogs are in 7-Elevens on the mainland. It rivals pizza as the local school cafeteria favorite. (In fact, the vast majority of the 261 island children who answered the *Honolulu Star-Bulletin*'s 1996 call for their depiction of an ideal Thanksgiving feast drew pictures of Spam musubi or pizza.) It was even served to the president of the United States during lunch at the Mid-Pacific Country Club on November 18, 1994, and, according to Ken Koike, club president at the time, Bill Clinton "thoroughly enjoyed" it.

To meet the needs of Spam musubi do-it-yourselfers, island drugstores sell

Mixed Media

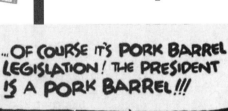

SPAM Fan... IF THE PRESIDENT OF THE UNITED STATES WAS A CAN OF SPAM...

SPAM Musubi

This recipe for Hawaii's popular sandwich-style Spam sushi is adapted from Ann Kondo Corum's *Hawaii's Spam Cookbook*.

1 (12-ounce) can Spam luncheon meat
Cooked Calrose (or other medium-grain, sticky) rice
Nori (seaweed, available at Asian markets)
Ume (pickled plum, available at Asian markets)

Cut Spam into 1/4-inch-thick rectangular slices and pan fry until brown. Shape cooked rice into blocks the length and width of the Spam slices and about 3/4 inch thick. (A plastic musubi maker will help with this if you have one. If not, pack the rice in the empty Spam can and then unmold it. Be careful, though, not to cut yourself on the sharp edges of the can.)

Spread some ume on one side of the rice and top with a slice of Spam. Cut nori into strips about an inch wide and long enough to wrap around the Spam-rice block widthwise. Lay Spam-rice block on top of one strip of nori, wrap, and eat. Ono!*

Deluxe variation: Scramble some eggs with a little sugar and soy sauce, cook like a frittata, cut into Spam-shaped rectangles, and place between rice and Spam.

*Hawaiian word for delicious!

acrylic Spam musubi–making boxes designed to press out cakes of rice in Spam slice dimensions. And to remind residents when to use those boxes, radio station KINE (105.1 FM) in Honolulu rings the island lunch bell every weekday at noon with "Spam Musubi," a "Y.M.C.A." parody written and performed by island comic Frank De Lima:

> *Hungry and I want something quick.*
> *Yes, I'm hungry, something two inches thick.*
> *Yes, I'm hungry, something shaped like a brick,*
> *Wrapped in clear, plastic Saran Wrap.*

Just how much Hawaiians love their Spam musubis is best understood by what happened in June 1994 when the state health department began enforcing long-standing regulations forbidding delis and convenience stores from selling perishable meat products—like Spam musubis—at room temperature.

Nothing less than Spamdamonium ensued. On local newspaper editorial pages and radio talk shows the debate raged: Food poisoning may be a legitimate public health issue, but to refrigerate rice is to ruin it. And as much as some people may think Spam is bad, nobody's ever heard of it *turning* bad. In 1996 a compromise was finally reached allowing Spam musubis to be left out at room temperature for up to four hours.

Musubis may be the most popular way to eat Spam in Hawaii, but they're only the beginning of its uses there. Most casual island restaurants also offer Spam saimin, a ramen-style soup featuring chopped Spam and vegetables, as well as bentos, box lunches consisting of a mound of rice, pickled ginger, and slices of fried chicken, mahi mahi, teriyaki beef, and Spam. These are usually served at noon, following the standard Hawaiian breakfast of Spam, eggs, and rice.

It's Ono-licious!

SPAM 'N' EGGS	1.95
SPAM MUSUBI	.75
SPAM SAIMIN	2.25
SPAM OMELET	2.00
SPAM WON TON	3/1.00
SPAM FRIED RICE	2.5

"It must be a local delicacy."

Island cook and cultural historian Ann Kondo Corum offers recipes for these and about forty-five other Spam dishes in her popular *Hawaii's Spam Cookbook.* Corum says Spam gained its place in island culture and cookery back in the early 1940s, when home refrigeration was new and fresh pork was hard to come by. Spam became the lunch of choice for plantation workers, she says, because it could be kept out in a hot field all morning without spoiling.

SPAM to the Rescue

Spam's virtual indestructibility puts it high on the wish lists of other folks, too, such as army supply sergeants, survivalists, campers, hermits—including Unabomber Ted Kaczynski, who reportedly stocked up on it on his infrequent trips to the grocery store—and disaster relief workers. Victims of hurricanes Hugo and Andrew, the San Francisco earthquake, and the Exxon oil spill all got fed Spam. Anthropologist Jane Goodall and her mother once made two thousand Spam sandwiches for Belgian troops fleeing from their African colony. And Cuban pitcher Orlando Hernández—the half brother of Florida Marlins star Livan—was able to pull off a dramatic December 1997 sea flight to freedom and land a $6.6 million contract with the New York Yankees in part because his leaky sailboat was stocked with drinking water, sugar, bread, and four cans of Spam.

Spam is also a much prized food bank donation and longtime staple of government food commodity programs for the poor. When the Salvation Army in Roxbury, Massachusetts,

Ann Kondo Corum

ran short of turkeys to give away in their Thanksgiving food bags in 1990, they substituted Spam. And Rayna Green, a Cherokee who directs the Smithsonian Institution's American Indian Program, remembers seeing it in government handouts of the postwar era and eating it in a Native American hominy dish that originally called for pork.

HiSPAMics

In a 1996 *People* magazine cover story, singer Gloria Estefan reminisced about the Coca-Cola glaze her mother made for the Spam that her family got at Miami's Freedom Tower, a processing center for refugees from Cuba. In nearby Puerto Rico, the favorite Spam dish is mixda, an hors d'oeuvre created by

smearing Spam with Cheez Whiz, placing it on Wonder bread, and cutting the bread into two-inch tea sandwiches. Spam also shows up as a filling at taco stands from East Harlem, New York, to Albuquerque, New Mexico.

So what is it with Spam and Hispanics? Beyond the role of government aid programs, the Spam number crunchers at Hormel Foods cite significant Spam-toting U.S. military populations in Puerto Rico and Cuba as well as Spam's compatibility with Hispanic food staples like rice and beans.

SPAM Sports

Of course, Spam love is not limited to eating. Younger Spam fans in particular seem to prefer other ways of incorporating it into

their active lifestyles. Take Stephen Craig, for example. He and some of his friends in Boulder, Colorado, built and raced a Spam vehicle in radio station KBCO's 1995 spring Kinetics Race. After donning pig ears, snouts, hooves, and tails, Craig and company pushed a papier-mâché pig-adorned Spammobile over land, mud, and water and onto victory as the team with the best theme. Overall, though, they came in only twelfth. In retrospect, Craig believes that bribing the judges with home-brewed beer bearing a Spam label could have been a misstep.

Even more physically demanding was the trip Mark Eppley and four friends made up Washington's Mount Rainier in the summer of 1996 under the moniker Team Spam. The name and the Spam

"Spam: The Other Pink Meat" was the official name of the vehicle Stephen Craig and company built and raced in Colorado.

gear were a tribute to Eppley's Minnesota roots. But those roots apparently are shallow: Eppley's published trip diary entries show him to be pining for a postclimb cheeseburger of the non-Spam variety!

Also falling into the Spam athletics category is the thirteen-mile San Diego "ride-and-tie" road and mountain bicycle race in which contestants

Right: The Spam stop on a San Diego road race. Below: Mark Eppley and the other members of Team Spam at the top of Mount Rainier.

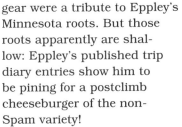

receive thirty-second time discounts for each piece of Spam they eat from a midcourse ironing board aid station. (Lest you read this as a Spam knock: Toting adorable toddler-sized teddy bears through the same race will cut a team's time by an even more impressive ten minutes.)

Eating Is Only the Beginning

Spam's delicious taste is only one of many reasons people love and buy the luncheon meat. Joey Green, author of *Polish Your Furniture with Pantyhose,* claims that Spam makes an excellent furniture polish as well as an antisteam agent for mirrors. Many fishermen, including a winner of the *Indianapolis Star*'s 1980 Big Fish Contest, recommend it as bait, especially if you're angling for catfish or carp. But Craig Yoder of Hemet Valley Medical Center in California gets the prize for buying Spam for the most unusual reason: to use as a magnetic resonance imaging (MRI) marker.

According to Yoder, doctors find it easier to spot abnormalities on MRIs if the problem area is outlined before the image is shot. Whereas some radiology technicians use Crisco or butter for this purpose, Yoder prefers to tape pellets of Spam to his patients because they show up better on the MRI and don't melt from body heat. In these days of rising medical costs, it's also worth noting that one twelve-ounce refrigerated block of Spam can yield up to two years' worth of MRI markers—assuming, of course, that the technician does not snack between patients.

An MRI of a slice of Spam.

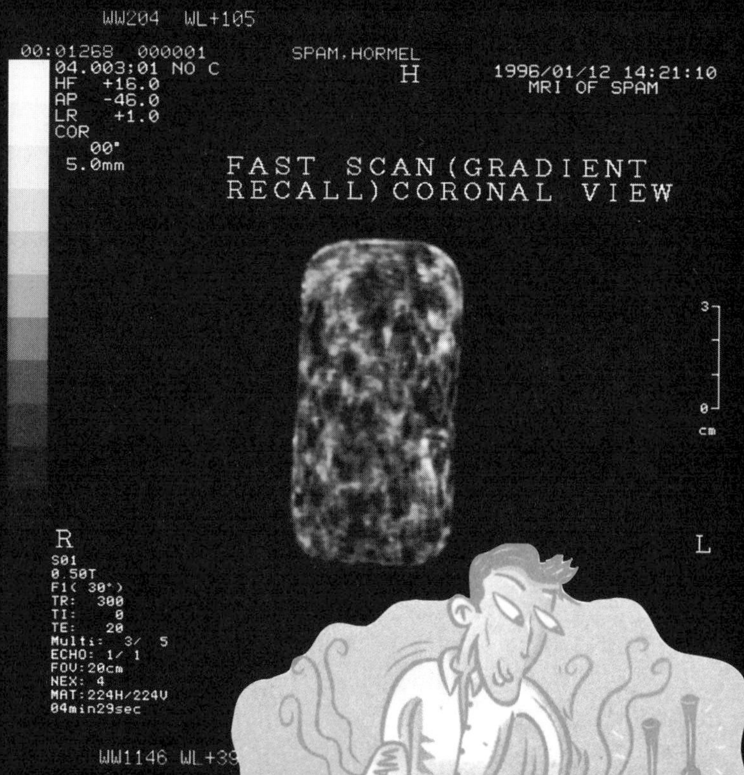

Why does Spam make a good furniture polish? According to Rutgers University food science professor Paul Lachance, the fat from the pork supplies the oil, and the meat proteins absorb stains.

SPAM Couture

Other people wear their love of Spam on their sleeves—literally. Lisa Heft, for instance, wore a Spam dress to a food-as-fashion party she helped organize as a benefit for the San Francisco Meals-on-Wheels program in 1984. To make it, Heft sliced up, slow-cooked, and shellacked the contents of ten cans of Spam, then attached them to a black shift like shingles for easy movement. Her accessories included Spam key earrings, a red pepper necklace, and a Carmen Miranda–style turban topped with a Spam can.

Of course it's one thing to wear Spam to a party and quite another to go to work every day dressed from head to toe in Spam gear. That's what Robert Taich (a.k.a. Mr. Spam) of Chicago did. A waiter at Ed Debevic's, a '50s diner that encourages its employees to come to work dressed in costume, Taich wore one or another of his Spam shirts, hats, and pants along with a Spam earring and watch for three years before passing his costume, Spam information sheets, and job on to friend Mark Smith. Ironically, though, neither Taich nor Smith could serve their customers Spam because it's not on Ed Debevic's menu.

Right: Robert Taich, the original Mr. Spam at Ed Debevic's in Chicago. Below: The Spam-stylish Lisa Heft.

Mike Seta of Cincinnati, a full-time graphic artist and part-time musician, decorated his electric guitar with epoxy-encased slices of Spam, "the miracle meat of many uses."

experimental physics at Cornell. The results of his experiment, which were published in Volume 33 (1993) of the journal *Cryogenics,* revealed that Spam conducts heat exactly the same as DuPont's Corian kitchen countertop. After leaving Cornell, where he also played Spam can maracas in a band called the Spam-Fisted Butchers of Jazz, Olson went on to a job at Los Alamos National Laboratory in New Mexico. A study of how Spam would stand up to a nuclear warhead should be forthcoming.

No boring white lab coat for Spam-loving physicist Jeffrey Olson.

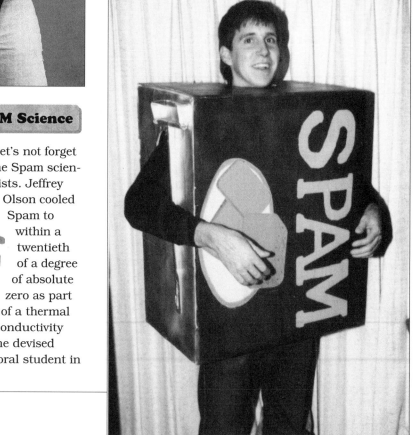

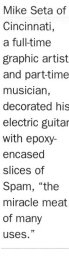

SPAM Science

And let's not forget the Spam scientists. Jeffrey Olson cooled Spam to within a twentieth of a degree of absolute zero as part of a thermal conductivity experiment he devised while a doctoral student in

Meating the Nonfood Needs of SPAM Eaters

In 1992, Hormel came up with a clever way to sell more Spam to people who can't seem to get enough of the luncheon meat as well as to those who like Spam more as concept than as cuisine: It began selling Spam T-shirts, watches, sweat suits, and the like.

The company had actually been fielding calls for years from consumers seeking to buy Spam artifacts created for sales or one-time promotions. Nevertheless, the first time it produced Spam merchandise for general commercial consumption and advertised it in a Sunday newspaper coupon insert, the response was overwhelming: seven thousand calls in two days. That didn't leave the folks there much time to sell luncheon meat and other food products. So in 1995 Hormel Foods decided to contract out its merchandising business to a direct-mail outfit.

DirectMark renamed the company's former gift catalog "Spamtastic" and raised both the prices of the goods and the hipness quotient. Out went the Spam tennis balls and the Hormel Foods barbecue tools; in came the moon-walk tees announcing "One small step for Spam" and the retro-chic baseball caps featuring Spam ads from the '40s. DirectMark also tried to capture the interest of collectors with die-cast Spam trucks and planes. But DirectMark President Mark Maddox believes the majority of the million-dollar business comes from cash-strapped fifteen- to twenty-five-year-olds who just want to have fun with the classic Spam T-shirts, Spam banks, Spam earrings, Spam neckties, and Spam-A-Rama bowling shirts that rack up the greatest sales.

Hormel Foods took the catalog back in house in 1998 and augmented its offerings with an extensive line of Spam baby wear—which only makes sense when you consider how crucial those first months and years of life are in shaping personality and taste.

Here's a Spampling of some of the most interesting Spam gear that's been introduced over the years:

SPAM BOXER SHORTS: Once sold en masse to groomsmen in a wedding party.

SPAM MOUSE PAD: Spam for a different kind of byting.

SPAM CANDY: Happily, just fruit- or mint-flavored hard candy in Spam-themed cellophane wrapping.

SPAM SNOWDOME: Nancy McMichael, owner of the country's largest snowdome collection, calls this her all-time favorite.

SPAM CAN AFGHAN: Just the thing Grandma might have made if she'd only understood you better.

SPAM CHRISTMAS STOCKING AND TREE ORNAMENTS: Ways to celebrate Christmas that the Wise Men never envisioned.

SPAM SANDALS: Make your mark as a Spam fan with these flip-flops that stamp "SPAM" where'er you roam.

SPAM BEACH CHAIR: When you think about it, sunbathers *are* a lot like Spam sizzling in a pan.

To check on current availability of these products or to receive the latest edition of the Spam catalog, call 1-800-LUV-SPAM.

SPAM Fan Extraordinaire

Chuck Hudson of Virginia Beach, Virginia, credits his transformation from ordinary Spam eater to extraordinary fan to a Spamposium he attended at the Colorado home of advertising man Lewis Cady in 1983 on the invitation of a mutual friend. After returning from it, the retired graphic artist put an old Spam key on his key ring, got an "MMSPAM" license plate for his car, and celebrated his fiftieth birthday at a brunch featuring Spam 'n' eggs and a three-by-five-foot ice carving of a Spam can. Hudson also has an account with a Virginia ham house that custom-smokes Spam for him in teriyaki, hickory, Old Bay, and garlic and pepper flavors.

However, the highlight of Hudson's Spam activities was undoubtedly his 1993 pilgrimage to the Hormel Foods plant in Austin, Minnesota. Thanks to an article in the *Virginian-Pilot* publicizing his love of

Members of the Chesapeake Bay Spam and Crab Society in full parade regalia.

Spam fan Chuck Hudson with the inspiration for his "MMSPAM" license plate and with his wife and daughter at the Spam factory in Austin, Minnesota.

Spam, Hudson and his wife and daughter got a private audience with then CEO Richard Knowlton and a plant tour normally reserved for VIPs. Hudson's voice trembles when he recalls being handed "a Spam can still warm from the cooker."

Hudson keeps that memory alive as a member of the Chesapeake Bay Spam and Crab Society, a club he formed in 1994 for people who like to sit around restaurants eating Spam and crab. Club members do push away from the table occasionally—to help judge the Spam-carving component of a local annual barbecue festival and to don pig-decorated paper-bag hoods for Norfolk's Friday-before-April-Fools'-Day Doo Dah Parade.

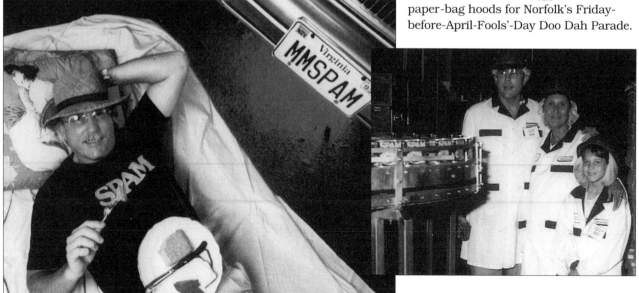

SPAM Fan Clubs

The Spam and Crab Society is actually just one of many ad hoc Spam fan clubs that have popped up across America. At Peet Junior High in Cedar Falls, Iowa, for instance, Mike Seeger and a group of "mainly bored, smart kids" started a Spam

Club to wrangle with members of the school's rival Treet Club. At South Plainfield High in New Jersey, a pseudoreligious society of fifty "Spamulists" created its own Web page and made four animated movies showing Spam cans battling soda bottles, candy wrappers, and competitive brands of luncheon meat. In Dallas, some party disc jockeys established a Spam support group of sorts, sending Spam Lite to any member on a diet and Spam Smoke Flavored to any member trying to give up smoking.

And in Bakersfield, California, twelve adults formed a Spam club after discovering a common childhood culinary love for the luncheon meat. When gourmet cooking with Spam no longer proved sufficiently amusing to the group, members began dressing up in Spam can costumes and visiting local supermarkets to rate the size and diversity of their Spam displays. Club activity peaked in the summer of 1988 when five members made the pilgrimage to Hormel headquarters. On the plane trip to Minnesota, they led passengers and crew in several choruses of their club song, "Turn, Turn, Turn Your Key" (sung to the tune of "Row, Row, Row Your Boat"), and after they arrived in Austin, they sang the same song to then Hormel President Knowlton while presenting him with a ten-inch gold Spam key.

The Official SPAM Fan Club

In 1998, Hormel Foods decided to formally recognize and organize these and other Spam-obsessed folks into an Official Spam Fan Club. For one-year dues of fifteen dollars and a willingness to "pledge to defend the good name of Spam luncheon meat, enjoy the great

Recommended Alcoholic Accompaniments to SPAM

BEER: An American pale ale such as Geary's or Sierra Nevada; or, if the Spam is charbroiled, an amber such as Samuel Adams Boston lager.

WINE: A fruity, slightly sweet wine such as a Riesling or a Gewürztraminer.

taste of Spam and spread the glad tidings of Spam to all corners of the sandwich," members receive an Official Spam Fan Club T-shirt, a membership certificate suitable for framing, a wallet-sized membership card, and the chance to see their Spam poems, pictures, and stories published in the quarterly club newsletter, *A Slice of Spam.*

The Official Spam Fan Club also recognizes achievements in Spam eating by bestowing elevated membership positions on those who can offer proof of purchase of twenty-five, fifty, or a hundred cans (which should give you an idea of the real interest that Hormel Foods has in all the Spam fun and games). The club's address is P.O. Box 892, Austin, MN 55912, and the phone number is 1-800-LUV-SPAM.

The World's Biggest SPAM Fan

The world's biggest Spam fan has yet to join the Official Spam Fan Club. In fact, no one has heard from him in quite some time. But Warren Johnson and the other hunter who had a close encounter with the creature in the Sierra Nevadas in 1971 are sure that he exists.

"We had gone to bed early and left some cooked Spam on the open-air stove," Johnson reported to the *Star* tabloid. "Sometime after dark we were awakened by a tremendous roaring, followed by groans and crashing. When it finally quieted, we went out for a look. We found the Spam gone," he said, and "two huge, 18-inch footprints." Spam fan Bigfoot? That's what Johnson and the *Star* believe.

'We talked to Bigfoot 40 times'

Selling SPAM

"George A. Hormel Had a Farm"

hink Spam luncheon meat is strange? Imagine how much more so it must have seemed when it was first introduced to the world in 1937, when (for the most part) meat did not come in a can, was not sold in grocery stores, and was not advertised on radio or in major magazines. If Jay Hormel had felt it necessary to spend the equivalent of a year of company profits to launch a cooked, canned version of a recognizable meat like ham, how much more would be required

to explain and create demand for a totally new, made-up meat like Spam?

Introducing the "Miracle Meat"

Introductory ads for Spam ran in major newspapers and women's magazines and stressed the "miracle" of a meat that "needs no pampering in the refrigerator," makes "any occasion more festive," and saves "kitchen work for thousands!" The ads featured several pairs of cartoon characters. One in each pair posed a question: "What's new in sandwiches?" "What's the treat for dinner?" "Maid's night out. What shall we eat?" The other answered every question with "Spam." Beside the dialogue bubbles, recipes

Background: The Hormel Girls performing sales troupe donned pig and cow masks for their big production number, "George A. Hormel Had a Farm."

The Original Recipe for Baked SPAM

Now a time-honored classic, this recipe for the clove-studded baked Spam pictured on the can until 1997 appeared in some of the earliest Spam ads.

1 (12-ounce) can Spam
    luncheon meat
Whole cloves
1/3 cup packed brown
    sugar
1 teaspoon water
1 teaspoon prepared mustard
1/2 teaspoon vinegar

Place Spam on rack in shallow baking pan; score surface and stud with cloves. In small bowl, combine brown sugar, water, mustard, and vinegar, stirring until smooth. Brush glaze over Spam. Bake 20 minutes at 375 degrees, basting often. Cut into slices. Serves 6.

cartoon-and-recipe format for years. The only major change was the introduction of rhyme, starting with the slogan "Cold or hot, Spam hits the spot" and expanding into cartoon balloon dialogue like this:

BOATING MAN: Lunch for captain and crew?
BOATING WOMAN: Aye, aye, sir! Spamwiches for two!

SLEEPY MAN: What's that sizzling sound I hear?
WIFE: Get up! It's Spam and eggs, my dear!

HAPPY HOUSEWIFE: Supper at six—don't be late!
DEPARTING HUSBAND: If you mean Spam—it's a date!

SPAM Gets a Life

The one big exception was the lengthy explication of the Spam story in a four-page advertising supplement to the November 1939 issue of *Life* magazine. Enclosed front and rear by pictures of those same parts of a hog, the supplement followed a pig on its journey from state fair to Hormel slaughterhouse to "fame" as the main ingredient in Spam, along the way introducing readers to a few of the hundreds of Austin, Minnesota, men and women who "have found steady employment in the cheerful surroundings of Hormel's Spam plant"—including "Spam maker" Darwin Howe.

"Off duty boner Howe, like most Spam makers," explained a side story about Howe and his family, "enjoys

suggested various ways of fixing the new "miracle meat" any time of the day or year.

Print ads retained essentially the same crammed

puttering about the house and garden," a fact documented by a photo of Howe and his wife with the caption "Mr. and Mrs. Howe putter." Two additional pictures showed the Howes' daughter, Kathleen, playing in a sandbox with other Hormel employee offspring, and the Howes' Spam-stuffed cupboard, "one of millions all over America, where housewives know that Spam is quick to prepare, needs no refrigeration, is always handy for breakfast, lunch or dinner."

The ad was obviously a soft sell, designed to make Spam seem as attractively American as apple pie, as familiar and unthreatening as the "blue-slacked" 4-H'er who, on the first page, "scrubbed her red pig in the white sunshine" of an "amazingly good county fair" in hopes of catching the eye of a Geo. A. Hormel & Company pig scout.

SPAM Hits the Airwaves

The first radio ads for Spam were similarly homespun, featuring these lyrics to the familiar "Bring Back My Bonnie to Me" in what is purported to be the first singing commercial:

> Spam, Spam, Spam, Spam
> Hormel's new miracle meat in a can
> Tastes fine, saves time

If you want something grand
Ask for Spam.

At the same time, the company lent Spam glamour by making it the primary sponsor of a new network radio variety show called *It Happened in Hollywood.* The show starred five unknowns discovered by Hormel scouts (presumably not the same ones who picked the pigs at country fairs) and told through song and skit of their struggles to make it in

Hollywood. As it turned out, those struggles came to life when Hormel dumped the show for another featuring the already established comics George Burns and Gracie Allen, along with band leader Artie Shaw.

SPAM Finds a "Meat-Heart"

Although *The George Burns and Gracie Allen Show* was sponsored by Spam, most of its on-air hawking seemed to come from the announcer, Jimmy Wallington. Hosts George and Gracie even joked about how abruptly and often Wallington managed to work in references to Spam.

"I love it here," Wallington declared during one of the show's frequent broadcasts from the road, in this case Chicago. "Actually I love it anywhere in these great United States. Spam is a wonderful product."

"Jimmy, isn't that a little off the subject?" protested George.

"No, it's a little off the pork shoulder with ham meat added,"

replied Wallington, before going into a Spam spiel capped by this chorus-sung ditty: "Slice it, dice it, fry it, bake it. Cold or hot, Spam hits the spot."

OUT OF THE BLUE FOR SPAM!

GRACIE ALLEN · GEORGE BURNS

WITH ARTIE SHAW AND HIS BAND

George and Gracie seemed a bit more involved with their canned meat sponsor off-mike. Promotional photos showed the couple posing with a pig named Spammy and Gracie (a.k.a. "Spam's meat-heart") trying to bake Spam in its can. Print ads mirrored the show's comic formula of George setting up Gracie's artfully literal responses. In one, George asks, "Gracie, next to pancakes, what do you like best?" Her answer, of course, is "Spam."

To support the Burns and Allen advertising, Hormel formed special Spam sales teams and, in selected cities, gave away money to every passerby who could produce a used Spam key. The combination of these efforts sent Spam sales soaring:

Burns and Allen ham it up with radio show mascot Spammy.

By 1940, 70 percent of urban Americans were eating Spam, compared to only 18 percent in 1937.

SPAM Gets Battle Fatigue

Ironically, the effectiveness of Hormel's early advertising and marketing of Spam actually backfired on the company after the United States entered World War II. Even though it was mostly government-formula luncheon meat, not Spam, that soldiers OD'd on during the war, they nevertheless associated all of it with the brand name that Hormel had made so familiar. In fact, Spam's wartime notoriety combined with shortages of other Hormel products to make many postwar consumers forget that Hormel produced anything but Spam.

To tackle that problem, and the equally vexing one of finding work for women employees who were returning from active duty in the military, Jay Hormel formed the Hormel Girls sales force of ex-servicewomen.

For God, Country, and SPAM

The sales force started out with just six women but soon grew to six-women crews that would visit grocers and entertain at Lions Club meetings. In addition to possessing "unquestioned character," musical talent, and sales ability, the GI Janes were required to join an all-female American Legion post that Jay helped to found in Austin. American Legion posts are normally named after people who have died for their country, but since no local women had been killed in the war and since almost half of the twenty founding members worked at Hormel, they asked headquarters if they could name their post after Spam. "Go ahead," came the reply, "As far as I'm concerned, Spam's deader'n hell anyway."

An active Legionnaire who began a tradition of supplying national convention paraders a free lunch of Spamwiches and milk in 1939, Jay Hormel now set his sights on turning his Hormel Girls sales group into the first all-female unit to participate in the August 1947 American Legion National Drum and Bugle Contest.

Spam Post 570 on the march in Racine, Wisconsin.

"It took a long time to find decent musicians who had also been GIs," recalls retired Hormel public relations director Stuart H. "Tate" Lane, who was in on the search to boost the group's numbers up to the requisite sixty. "They never were truly great." Nevertheless, the women were found and shipped off to a military academy in Connecticut for five weeks of eleven-hour days of bugling, drumming, and marching—interrupted only by a move to a more remote drilling location when neighbors sued over the noise.

The "All GI Girls Spam Post 570," as the banner preceding them on the parade route proclaimed, did not win the contest. But they did provide the nucleus for the group that would carry out Jay's next big idea: a Hormel-sponsored nationwide radio show whose stars would double as traveling saleswomen. This time, the GI requirement was dropped because Hormel needed women musically versatile enough to form an orchestra of twenty-four, a chorus of thirty-six, and a band of sixty.

A SPAMtastic Show

For the next five years, people from across America turned on their radios to these words: "Hello, may we join you? It's *Music with the Hormel Girls*." The show consisted of Broadway show tunes and current hits interspersed with skits and an extraordinary number of product references. Whereas a typical half-hour radio drama in those days carried three commercials, *Music with the Hormel Girls* featured five—with

I AM YOUR LUCKY HORMEL GIRL

processed became a dirty word in the food industry.

Road Food

A typical visit to a town began with the Hormel Girls' caravan of thirty-five white Chevrolets and five equipment trucks pulling into town with a police escort, followed by a welcoming ceremony attended by the city's mayor and sometimes even the governor. If that didn't draw a crowd, then the parade that usually took place later would.

In those days the sight of sixty women doing anything together without men was enough to create a

an additional fifteen references to Hormel products worked into the script. Even before the first commercial aired on the April 17, 1948, show, for example, banter about a man whose "girl couldn't cook" ended with the suggestion that the man be given a coupon for Hormel chili con carne, and the Hormel Girls treated the audience to "Spamoem Time" by reciting a poem about Spam that they had supposedly written in their spare time.

The shop talk on the program probably seemed natural to the girls because they spent most of their nonperforming moments selling Spam and other Hormel products. The caravan newsletter, *Oink Oink,* prepared to answer any questions grocers or consumers might pose. "It is a company policy to deliver merchandise to the consumer as fully processed as possible. Canned meats represent the ultimate in food processing," intoned an article in one issue—obviously written decades before

stir—and sometimes even a suspicion. Ex–Hormel Girl Mary Ellen Domm still remembers one old man's reaction to seeing the caravan stop at his Texas gas station the morning after a nearby border town's red-light district had burned down: "They burn them out there and now they come out over here."

The girls, who spent their afternoons canvassing and couponing door-to-door—in teams of two in case of vicious dogs or men who answered the door naked, as once happened—had to live within a strict set of company-imposed rules. "You never appeared in public other than in complete control and with lady-like demeanor," recalls former Hormel Girl Laverne Wollerman. "We carried his name, you see."

SPAM Daddy Meats the Caravan

"His name" was Jay Hormel, company president, and Jay took great personal interest in the show. More than once he appeared unannounced wherever the caravan had stopped so that he could have dinner with the girls and watch the show. More than once before the radio show became well known, he also drove some business associates to the outskirts of a town where the caravan was scheduled to appear and bet them that thirty-five white Chevys carrying sixty women would soon be coming round the bend. Naturally, he always won.

"He loved the caravan, the girls, the whole idea of it," recalls Domm. But Hormel Vice President Park

Spending on SPAM

In 1996, Hormel Foods spent $6.3 million advertising Spam. According to Competitive Media Reporting, that's a full 75 percent of the total spent on advertising for *all* canned meats, chicken, and fish that year, and it's nearly 70

A lot of meat. But not a lot of money.

times the amount the Dial Corporation put out to advertise its entire line of Armour Star canned meat products, including Treet. And Spam's advertising budget increased to $10 million in 1998. If you've ever wondered why Spam sells more than seven times better than Treet and commands 60 percent of America's luncheon meat market, here's one possible reason.

. . . with every Used Car!

Dougherty apparently did not. From his point of view, says Domm, it was too expensive. There had been a precedent for the Hormel Girls' approach to marketing in the Chili Beaners, a twenty-member Mexican song-and-dance troupe that toured midwestern fairs promoting Hormel chili in 1935. But that was only twenty people traveling in one section of the country during fair season. The Hormel Girls had more than three times the personnel eating, staying in hotels, and driving an average of thirty thousand miles a year. Plus there was the cost of putting on a national radio show. On the other hand, sales of Hormel packaged foods more than doubled during the years the Hormel Girls were on the road.

In the end, it was probably not money but the faltering health of troupe booster Jay and the dawn of television that led to the group's disbanding in December 1953 and Hormel's return to a more conventional sales approach of magazine advertisements featuring recipes.

Rosie Returns to the Kitchen

The Spam recipes that appeared in ads just after the war read like remedial cooking lessons for all the Rosie the Riveters who were returning to their kitchens. "Make Spamwich of sliced Spam and cheese. Serve with chips and raw vegetables such as carrots in long slices, radishes, green onions, peppers, celery. Variation: Spread mustard or meat sauce on Spam, then toast."

But by the end of the Hormel Girls' reign, the Hormel test kitchens were able to assume an audience of housewives comfortable enough with postwar convenience food cooking to be able to churn out a molded Spam 'n' rice ring and Creole- or Hawaiian-style "Spam-dandy skillet suppers."

"Happy Meat"

Most of these recipe ads appeared in such major women's publications as *Woman's Day*, *Family Circle*, and *Ladies' Home Journal*. But in 1962 Hormel redirected a major chunk of its

"Life with Father is lots more fun since we found **SPAM**"

... Says Mrs. Keith Holton of Evanston, Ill.

MY HUSBAND used to be pretty grumpy in the morning ... but all that's changed now. You ought to see him light up when I bring on the SPAM & Eggs! It's our favorite breakfast.

Dear Mrs. Holton:

Thanks for your nice words. We who help make SPAM honestly believe it's the finest product of its kind . . . . a delicious blend of juicy-sweet pork shoulder and tender, tasty ham meat.

Gertrude Nelson

of the SPAM family

A Decade of Unparalleled Innovation in the SPAM Kitchens

The creativity of Hormel home economists may have peaked in the "lovely to look at—luscious to eat!" Spam recipes they developed for magazine ads during the 1950s. Here is a "delicious, picture-pretty" sampling.

SPAM 'n' Banana Fritters

1 (12-ounce) can Spam luncheon meat
4 bananas with green tips
1 egg, beaten
$1/3$ cup milk
$1/2$ teaspoon fat, melted
$1/2$ cup flour, sifted
$1/2$ teaspoon salt
$1/2$ teaspoon baking powder

Cut Spam into $1/8$ to $1/4$-inch slices. Cut bananas in quarters lengthwise. Combine egg with milk and fat. Into this mixture stir flour, salt, and baking powder to form a batter. Dip bananas in batter. Pan fry in $1/2$ inch hot fat in skillet with Spam slices until brown. Serve hot.

Lovely to look at—luscious to eat!

Party SPAMwich Loaf

1 unsliced square loaf of sandwich bread
Butter
Mayonnaise
Chicken
Lettuce
Tomatoes, sliced
Ripe olives, chopped
1 (12-ounce) can Spam luncheon meat, sliced
Heavy cream, stiffly whipped
Hard-boiled eggs, chopped

Remove crust from bread. Cut bread lengthwise into four slices and butter each slice. Top first layer with mayonnaise, chicken, and lettuce; second layer with tomatoes and olives; third layer with mayonnaise, Spam, and lettuce. Cover with top layer of bread.

Mix mayonnaise, whipped cream, and chopped eggs together in bowl. Use mixture to frost entire loaf. Chill in refrigerator 3 to 5 hours. To serve, cut across loaf into thick slices.

Fruit Cocktail–SPAM Buffet Party Loaf

This paragon of eating excess—which combines Spam with such other equally important '50s food staples as fruit cocktail, gelatin, and Miracle Whip—comes from a 1954 Del Monte ad.

1 (15-ounce) can Del Monte fruit cocktail, drained (reserve syrup)
2 tablespoons unflavored gelatin
2 tablespoons vinegar
$1/2$ teaspoon ground cinnamon
$1/8$ teaspoon ground cloves
2 (12-ounce) cans Spam luncheon meat, very finely chopped
$1/2$ cup celery, very finely chopped
$1/4$ cup green olives, very finely chopped
$1/2$ cup Miracle Whip
1 teaspoon prepared mustard
$1/2$ teaspoon salt
5 lemons
Paprika
Additional Miracle Whip

Arrange drained fruit cocktail in 9-by-5-by-3-inch loaf pan. In top of double boiler, mix reserved syrup with gelatin, vinegar, cinnamon, and cloves. Place over hot water and stir until gelatin dissolves. Carefully pour $1/2$ cup of gelatin mixture over fruit cocktail. Place pan in refrigerator and chill until gelatin has thickened but is not set.

Mix Spam with celery and olives. Mix Miracle Whip with mustard, salt, and remaining gelatin mixture. Add Spam mixture to Miracle Whip mixture and blend well. Spread over fruit cocktail. Chill until firm, at least 4 hours.

For garnish, make lemon cups by

halving lemons, slicing off ends (so lemons will stand up), and scooping out pulp. Dip cut edges of lemons in paprika. Fill cups with Miracle Whip and sprinkle lightly with additional paprika.

To serve, unmold loaf onto large platter and surround with lemon cups. Makes 8 to 10 servings.

Spam advertising to teen magazines like *Seventeen* and *Ingenue*. The first wave of baby boomers had hit adolescence, and in hopes of getting them into the Spam habit, Hormel advertisers transformed Spam into "happy meat," an "after-the-game party pleaser" not just "fun to make" and "fun to eat" but "fun to feed to hungry boyfriends." They also launched a

Please don't eat the radio!

Turn on with our Psyche-deli SPAMwich—a wild combination of thin-sliced SPAM, Swiss cheese and sauerkraut with a touch of mayonnaise. Then tune in our seven-transistor SPAM Radio Offer. Just send us five dollars cash or money order with this coupon. Allow 30 days delivery.

SPAM RADIO $5.00
Box 772, Maple Plain, Minnesota 55359

Here's my $5.00. Tune me in with my own transistorized, take-along SPAM can radio.

Name_____

Address_____

City_____State_____Zip_____
Offer expires December 31, 1969.

SPAM is a pure pork product .... ly by Geo. A. Hormel & Co.

'Easy, son—your Uncle Joe and I haven't had <u>seconds</u> on SPAM yet."

"Spamaroo" rhyming contest that dangled Bobbie Brooks clothes, Tangee makeup travel cases, Presto portable hair dryers, and Smith-Corona typewriters as prizes. Two of the winning entries in the contest focused on Spam's usefulness as boy bait:

> *When your pigeon's roaming,*
> *Spam will keep him homing.*

> *Cleopatra with feminine guile,*
> *Said to Tony, "Let's barge down the Nile!"*
> *Then she packed up some Spam,*
> *Bags of popcorn and jam,*
> *To beguile him down the Nile*
> *In high style.*

A third emphasized its appeal to a new generation:

> *In this day of hippies and space,*
> *I eat Spam to keep up with the pace.*

IT'S A SPAM SUMMER!

The World according to SPAM Marketers

Spam marketers divide the world into three categories of people:

SPAM USERS: This third of the population includes minorities in all demographic categories; young, frequently none-too-wealthy southern families; and oldsters who ate Spam during World War II and Korea. Unfortunately, those in the last group are either dying out or being put on fat- or sodium-restricted diets that force them to eat Spam infrequently or not at all.

People who do eat Spam do so first and foremost because of its unique taste, says Thomas Keating, vice president and management supervisor for the product at Batten, Barton, Durstine & Osborn advertising agency. Most also have some kind of nostalgic feeling for the food. "For a lot of people, Spam brings up very, very positive memories of growing up, when life was simpler

and they didn't have the kind of worries they do now—memories of having Spam for breakfast before going off fishing with their dad, for instance." In fact, Keating says, members of Spam marketing focus groups sometimes get close to weeping when reminiscing about Spam.

Keepability and versatility are tied as the next two most-often-cited reasons for buying the luncheon meat.

NEUTRAL NONUSERS: This 40 to 45 percent of the population doesn't eat Spam but doesn't really have anything against it, either. Neutral nonusers represent Hormel Foods' best chance of boosting Spam sales in the United States.

NEGATIVE NONUSERS: Unfortunately for Hormel Foods, the war veteran fans of Spam are rapidly being replaced by this quarter of the population. Negative nonusers are mainly young and well educated—except about canned meats, which they automatically assume to be inferior to fresh. Many can't believe anyone actually eats Spam, and they themselves buy it only on rare occasions in the spirit of experimentation or fun. To them, Spam is a remnant of an earlier era of eating in America, a cultural relic, a source of endless amusement and speculation— but not a serious foodstuff.

Magazine editors trying to keep up with the convenience food craze (or perhaps just simply smart enough to know which side of their bread was covered with Spam) also worked it into their columns. One such column in *Woman's Day,* a piece entitled "How to Be

a Girl," began by urging teens to "Start making your reputation as a cook right now!" and featured a recipe for a concoction called Chick-Ham à la Princesse with cubed Spam, canned cream of chicken soup, and evaporated milk.

To reinforce its advertising campaign in the teen market, Hormel prepared and sent out packages of "educational" materials ostensibly about meal planning to home economics teachers in high schools around the country. "Students in your class may or may not have tried Spam," the teacher's guide acknowledged, "but the attractive photographs on the wallchart will probably make them take an interest and some discussion of the product is in order." Another section of the guide advised teachers to "prepare as many as possible of the recipes . . . below."

The Bologna Wars

In the early 1970s, high meat prices caused by a meat shortage and Spam's dominance of its own luncheon meat category inspired Spam marketers to try to lure consumers away from bologna. The new series of television ads began by showing the same dollar value of bologna and Spam being stacked on opposite sides of a scale and ended—naturally—with the Spam side plunging downward. Another series made the same point by showing how many more sandwiches could be made with a dollar's worth of Spam than with a dollar's worth of

bologna. All ended with a disembodied hand plopping coins into a Spam bank and a disembodied voice (in some cases, the one associated with Wilma of *The Flintstones*) reciting the slogan "A lot of meat. But not a lot of money."

The SPAMpire Campaign

Spam's great taste took center stage in the next wave of Spam ads. Launched in 1980, the "Love at First Bite" campaign offered to refund the price of a can of Spam to anyone who tried it and didn't like it. Echoing the Mikey commercials for Life cereal, one "Love at First Bite" ad featured a wife nervously serving Spam to her husband for the first time.

"He likes it!" she declares after observing his pleased reaction.

"Like it? I love it!" he corrects.

"You can relax, Hormel," the wife concludes, referring to the money-back guarantee.

If Hormel was able to relax, it wasn't for long. The campaign was discontinued after only a year. Official advertising histories say it was because the 1979 Dracula comedy *Love at First Bite* objected to

Python's Flying Circus and elsewhere. The so-called "Surprise" campaign recorded actual reactions of people caught in the act of eating Spam. In one ad, there's speculation about a Spam animal. In another, a woman tries it, finds out what it is, then says, "Delicious. I'm going to make it for a party, but I'll hide the can." The tag line was the modest "Spam. It just might surprise you."

In keeping with the irreverent style of the ads and the age of the people Hormel was trying to reach, the "Surprise" campaign was launched on major-market rock-and-roll radio stations. Later, when it moved into print, it included a magazine contest that challenged readers to identify a blind-folded celebrity Spam lover (Bernie Koppell, a.k.a. Doc from *The Love Boat*).

Hormel's use of the phrase and not—as some Spam scoffers might suspect—because of an avalanche of refund requests.

The SPAM Animal and Other Surprises

Nevertheless, the company's next advertising campaign acknowledged the ribbing Spam was getting on *Monty*

Although at first a tough sell with Hormel executives, the "Surprise" ads tested well with focus groups, won industry awards, and prompted free publicity in the form of newspaper articles and a *Today* show segment. The one speculating about a Spam animal also inspired many amateur renditions and at least one professional one from *Far Side* cartoonist Gary Larson.

Different SPAMs for Different Folks

Hormel Foods has never taken David Letterman up on his suggestion that it produce Spam-on-a-rope. However, over the years the company has introduced new versions of Spam to keep the luncheon meat up with the changing times. For those of you boning up for the Spam category sure to appear one of these days on *Jeopardy,* here's the chronology:

1962: Seven-ounce Spam debuts for singles and smaller families.

1964: News of consumers who put their Spam through a meat grinder leads to Deviled Spam Spread. When the Department of Agriculture modifies its definition of *deviled* in 1970, the name changes to Spam Spread.

1971: Hormel creates Spam with Cheese Chunks and Spam Smoke Flavored in response to new smoked and maple versions of competitor Treet. (Barbecue and butter maple flavors of Spam are also tested but never released.) Looking like an orange polka-dotted version of the original pink brick, Spam with Cheese Chunks is introduced with an animated ad showing mice unsuccessfully trying to get into the can. Potential human consumers are less enthusiastic, and the product is discontinued. Spam Smoke Flavored is still produced but is carried by only about a quarter of American supermarkets.

1986: Responding to growing consumer concern about nutrition, Hormel launches 25% Less Salt/Sodium Spam. Introductory ads wink at the previous year's New Coke controversy by featuring a picture of a full Coke glass and the caption "Another American favorite has changed its formula. But we still have Classic Spam." About 20 percent of all Spam consumers now choose reduced-sodium Spam, probably more for its less salty taste than for health reasons. The product's own label warns that it is "not recommended for sodium-restricted diets."

1990: Spam comes out of the can and into the refrigerator case as Spam Breakfast Strips. The product is designed to appeal to younger consumers who are not comfortable with canned meat, but those same consumers seem equally uncomfortable with pink bacon that has a shelf life of 120 days. Spam Breakfast Strips never get out of initial test markets.

1992: Hormel goes national with Spam Lite, which contains 25 percent less fat and calories than regular Spam (upped to 50 percent less fat and 33 percent fewer calories when new regulations redefining the word *lite* come into effect in 1994). The company achieves the savings not by putting its hogs on diets but by adding chicken to the traditional pork (Spam Lite contains no ham). Despite some joking—one food critic calls Spam Lite "an oxymoron," another enshrines it in his Foolish Foods Hall of Fame—Spam Lite is partially credited for a brand sales spike of 10 percent that year and now accounts for 15 to 20 percent of all Spam sales. Households favoring it tend to be smaller and either younger or older than those buying regular Spam.

1995: Spam Lite becomes available in a seven-ounce can. An eighteen-ounce can of regular Spam proves to be too much of a good thing even in Spam-loving Hawaii, the only place it is sold before going the way of Spam bacon.

1997: After two years in the food lab, a 96-percent-fat-free version of Spam is introduced in six test markets. Made from oven-roasted white turkey meat, this new-age Spam contains only two grams of fat per two-ounce serving.

SPAM on Wheels

SPAMmin' through the Reagan Years

The mid-'80s produced two interesting burps in the history of ads encouraging people to digest Spam. "Dress Up Spam" borrowed the California Raisins' Claymation techniques to make Spam seem fun and contemporary. While showing, among other dazzling things, a Spam submarine sandwich turning into a real submarine, sinking into the ocean, and then re-emerging as a couple of Spam cans, the ad effectively dramatized Spam's versatility.

Commenting as much on the lifestyles and values of the era as on the gustatory allurements of Spam, an ad from 1985's "Out of the Blue" campaign depicted the hectic life of a supposedly typical American family in which Dad assumes at least a portion of the meal-making and laundry duties. While Mom takes a business call and Sis dribbles a basketball to the rhythm of driving, highly percussive background music, Dad has an inspiration that solves the food part of the family's frenzy. "Spamburger" appears in a thought bubble by his head as an unseen chorus chants:

> *The family's busy, so are you.*
> *Got to eat fast,*
> *What can you do?*
> *Spam, it came to me right out of the blue.*

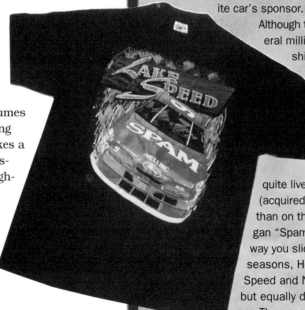

SPAM® At High Speed.

In 1995 Spam joined Vermont Teddy Bears, World Championship Wrestling, the Hooters restaurant chain, and Budget Gourmet TV dinners in the list of most unlikely sponsors of a racing car. Hormel Foods executives made the decision based not only on the fantastic growth of interest in stock car racing, especially among southern women, who are Spam's biggest actual and potential consumers, but also on the amazing brand loyalty shown by fans of the National Association of Stock Car Auto Racing (NASCAR)—with up to 71 percent saying that they buy the products of their favorite car's sponsor.

Although the company invested several million dollars in its sponsorship of the No. 9 Melling Racing Thunderbird, otherwise known as the Spam car, and in a whole catalogful of related merchandise, driver Lake Speed never quite lived up either to his name (acquired in the bassinet rather than on the racetrack) or to the slogan "Spam Racing: A winner any way you slice it." After two dismal seasons, Hormel Foods dumped Speed and No. 9 in favor of a new but equally disappointing driver and car. The second time, though, the company waited only half a season before bowing out of its deal with Mike Wallace and his No. 91 Chevrolet Monte Carlo. The result? Tons of Spam racing shirts, caps, and jackets available at bargain-basement prices.

In the mid-1990s, the Minnesota Moose hockey team put Spam on ice.

WE LIKE **SPAM** BURGERS A LOT!

1940. In an old "Spam Hits the Spot" print ad featuring the Joseph Havstad family of Minneapolis, Mrs. Havstad declares, "Our favorite summer sport is making Spamburgers on our outdoor grill."

Lang's eurekalike contribution to this age-old idea was to suggest making the Spamburgers by cutting off the square side of the Spam loaf rather than the rectangular side, as had been done—and shown on the can—for Spam's entire history. Two such chops to a standard twelve-ounce can would create three quarter-pound burgers in the same shape seen at White Castle and Wendy's. And in the

SPAMburger, SPAMburger, SPAMburger

Spam's next important campaign, launched in 1992, was the result of a directive from Hormel President Joel Johnson to longtime ad agency Batten, Barton, Durstine & Osborn (BBDO) of Minneapolis: make Spam part of the everyday lives of Americans again rather than just something they keep on the shelf in case of emergencies. BBDO Art Director Paul Lang is credited with coming up with the answer—or rather the questions that provided the basis for the campaign: Why are hamburgers called hamburgers when they don't contain any ham? Wouldn't it make more sense to make a hamburger out of a meat that actually contains ham—like Spam, for instance?

Of course it would. In fact, Lang's own agency had used the idea as recently as 1985 and as far back as 1939 or early '90s, fast food was big competition for supermarket convenience food.

The fast-paced, high-energy television ads launching the idea depicted Spam lovers from sea to shining sea. But like the ads in the "Surprise" campaign, they did not overpromise. In fact, most of them began with a disheveled businessman taking a bite of a Spamburger and saying only that it "tastes pretty good." Although he concludes that "Spam's made from ham, right? So really, this is a hamburger," he nevertheless appears to have to struggle with the news that he has just eaten Spam.

The public was less skeptical, sending Spam volume sales soaring 11 and 17 percent, respectively, for the two quarters of 1992 and 1993 when the Spamburger concept was introduced. To celebrate,

A Texas cowgirl demonstrates the Spamburger cut in this TV ad.

Two-time National Football League MVP and Super Bowl™ XXXI Champion Brett Favre, enjoys a delicious **SPAMBURGER®** **Hamburger**, a hot & hearty bowl of **HORMEL® Chili** and a tall glass of wholesome milk.

Hormel created a special limited-edition Spam can with a picture of a Spamburger in place of the vintage baked Spam with cloves.

SPAMily Values

A few years later, in the mid-'90s, Hormel Foods launched another new campaign clearly designed to appeal to the millions of overworked Americans longing for a slower, simpler, and more meaningful lifestyle. Consisting of mood pieces featuring cute kids roughhousing with their siblings and parents, including many of African-American and Hispanic heritage, the "I Like Spam" ads focused on the important things in life, like spending time with your family—and eating Spam, of course. As one verse of the accompanying music put it:

I like bread and butter.
I like toast and jam.
I like the good and simple things.
That's why I like Spam.

Thoroughly Modern SPAM

The first new Spam advertising campaign of 1997 echoed the "Surprise" campaign in acknowledging some of the jokes about

Spam. "Okay, so the name's funny. But there's nothing funny about the taste," read one that appeared in *Soap Opera Digest* and—in a first for Spam advertising—tabloids like the *Star* and the *National Enquirer*. ("Our users are reading these publications," Spam brand manager Jim Splinter explains.)

Later in 1997, Hormel Foods celebrated Spam's sixtieth birthday by giving it a snazzy new polypropylene label—with a contemporary-looking Spamburger in place of the old clove-studded loaf—and coming up with a complementary new ad concept, the disappearing Spamburger. In "So good . . . it's gone" print ads, the image of the Spamburger disappears off the can. In a companion TV ad, the real thing is stolen by a clever criminal: Just as Dad is getting ready to bite into a Spamburger, baby throws a rattle to distract him. While Dad is busy retrieving the rattle, baby moves in on the Spamburger. When the ad ends, Dad is staring at an empty plate and baby is emitting a telltale burp of Spamisfaction.

So good...

...it's gone.™

www.spam.com

A Fair Test of SPAM Cooking Prowess

After more than sixty years, are there really any new and interesting ways to prepare Spam? In recent years, Hormel Foods home economists who struggle daily with this question in the service of greater Spam sales have received some aid from the annual state fair Best Spam Recipe Contest. Since its 1991 debut at twenty fairs, the contest has grown to include more than twelve hundred participants at more than seventy fairs across the country. Officials at Hormel Foods say it only goes to prove how popular Spam is. However, prizes that are among the most lucrative on the state fair circuit probably also have something to do with it. "For most food contests you might get three or four dollars and a ribbon. But the first-prize winner gets a hundred dollars in The Spam," says Florence Dixon of South Haven,

Ruth Parsons' Spam Fireball Spread won first place at the Delaware State Fair in 1995.

Mississippi, using the term everyone she knows uses for the Best Spam Recipe Contest. "It's amazing what money will make you think about," she says.

Amazing, indeed, when you consider some of the fare The Spam has inspired: Spam mincemeat pie, something called 24-Carat Spam Macadamia Nut Mousse, even Spam ice cream. And these are just the winners! One losing concoction at the 1995 New Mexico State Fair, called Sun of Spam, featured a fan of Spam wedges trimmed with green olives and crushed pineapple in the center of a bowl of yellow Jell-O.

All of the recipes that win first prize at local fairs are tested in the kitchens of Hormel Foods by Debbie VanDenBerg, who makes and tastes Spam dishes at a rate of six to ten per day. How can a contestant be sure his or her Best Spam Recipe entry pleases VanDenBerg's palate?

SPAM Bread

You can hardly taste the Spam in this banana-bread-like award winner from the 1993 Stephenson County Fair in Illinois. We'll let you decide whether that's good or bad.

1/3 cup sugar
1/4 teaspoon cinnamon
2 medium unpeeled apples, cored and seeded
3/4 cup raisins
1 (12-ounce) can Spam luncheon meat
3 1/4 cups all-purpose flour, sifted
1 3/4 cups sugar
1/2 teaspoon salt
1 teaspoon cinnamon
3/4 cup cooking oil
1/2 teaspoon baking powder
2 eggs
3/4 teaspoon baking soda

3/4 cup buttermilk
3/4 cup chopped pecans plus 1/8 cup pecan halves

Mix sugar and cinnamon in a small cup. Cover sides and bottom of two 8-by-4 1/2-inch glass loaf pans with non-stick shortening spray. Sprinkle sides and bottoms with cinnamon-sugar mixture.

Coarsely grind apples, raisins, and Spam. Set aside. Put flour, sugar, salt, cinnamon, cooking oil, baking powder, eggs, baking soda, and buttermilk in a mixing bowl and beat until smooth. Stir in Spam, apples, raisins, and chopped pecans.

Pour into prepared pans. Bake at 325 degrees for 30 minutes. Decorate tops of loaves with pecan halves. Turn oven temperature up to 350 degrees and bake for another 30 minutes until tops are brown or a toothpick inserted in centers comes out clean.

Linda Cole enjoys a whiff of her award-winning Spam-stuffed peppers—apparently unaware that she is about to be struck by a can of Spam Lite.

Follow these slices of advice from her as well as from Spam contest organizers and winners:

❑ Look through the Spam recipe books put out by Hormel Foods so you aren't duplicating old dishes.

❑ Keep the recipe simple—under seven ingredients and thirty minutes' preparation time, if possible. "People are busy. They haven't got the time to get really involved in a recipe—and if they *are* going to spend that kind of time, they're [not] going to use . . . a convenience product like Spam," says VanDenBerg.

❑ "Find a recipe that everyone loves that can be adapted to Spam. That's the key," says Florence Dixon, who won first prize as well as Best of Show at 1994's Mid-South Fair by modifying a recipe for chipped beef. Jette Robinson did the same with her favorite manicotti recipe in 1995 and won the national grand prize.

❑ Taste accounts for only 40 percent of the Best Spam Recipe judging points. Don't forget appearance (30 percent) and originality (30 percent). To win the national award in 1993, Linda Cole used peppers of three different colors in her Spam-stuffed peppers recipe and presented them on an attractive plate of the right size. Cole says it's also good if you can "pick up on a new food trend," especially if you can give it some kind of twist. In her case the trend was healthier eating, so her recipe contains Spam Lite and lots of fresh vegetables.

SPAM Scargot

This takeoff on the classic French snail dish won a blue ribbon at the 1996 Ventura County Fair, Ventura, California.

1 (12-ounce) can Spam luncheon meat
$1/2$ pound butter, softened
2 tablespoons chopped shallots
2 tablespoons chopped green onions
1 teaspoon garlic salt
5–6 tablespoons chopped parsley
12 super-clean escargot shells
$1/2$ cup bread crumbs

Cut Spam into cubes or shape into balls and lightly brown in a little of the butter. Cream together softened butter, shallots, green onions, garlic salt, and parsley.

Place shells in an escargot pan. Put some butter-shallot mixture in each shell. Put a Spam cube or ball in each shell. Top with remaining butter mixture and bread crumbs. Bake at 450 degrees until butter sizzles, about 10 to 20 minutes. Yields 12 appetizers.

SPAM Around the Globe

ountries in the European and Pacific theaters faced major challenges in rebuilding following World War II—including coping with the fact that they now had Spam luncheon meat. Not only did the U.S. military's overuse and abuse of Spam not kill the postwar American market for the product; it actually opened up whole new markets overseas.

In a sense, U.S. military and lend-lease programs served as unpaid Spam salesmen. Spam spread, and caught on, particularly in places with iffy electricity and poor food distribution systems. Potted pork products may be a joke to the time-pressed, natural-food-obsessed, Boston-Market-chicken-eating yuppies who represent the future of the food industry in the United States, but in many other places around the world,

canned meats like Spam are all that stands between people and a week in bed with food poisoning. Furthermore, fat grams that have been Spam's nemesis in the United States are not usually as great a concern to people in less industrialized societies, who worry more about getting enough calories from *any* source to fuel a hard day's manual labor.

Add these factors to the prestige that Spam shares with Levi's and McDonald's hamburgers in many foreign countries just because it comes from trend-setting America and it's not hard to understand why the greatest per capita consumption of Spam and the greatest possibilities for its future as a foodstuff now lie outside its continental U.S. homeland. Currently a little more than a third of all Spam, or fifty million cans a year, is sold overseas.

Richard Crane, a former Spam brand manager who is now marketing and sales manager for Hormel Foods International, says the best foreign markets for Spam have one or more of the following characteristics: a high current or former U.S. military presence, a population with a taste for pork products, and extremes in weather—typically a hot climate.

South Korean Chic

Not surprisingly, South Korea, a place where Spam is considered to be a gourmet treat, has all three characteristics. University of the Pacific anthropologist George Lewis believes the Spam-like qualities of the traditional Korean dish *you yuk*—which is made by pressing boiled beef or pork into a loaf and then cutting it into slices—may have also paved the way for Spam's acceptance there. In any case, Spam is featured in a variety of Korean dishes, including soups, elegant sushi rolls called kimpap, and stir-fries with the spicy pickled vegetable condiment kimchi.

Spam came to Korea during the Korean War and was introduced to civilians by a military-base black

Korean-Style SPAM

Ann Kondo Corum includes this recipe from Lloyd Pak for Korean-style Spam in her *Hawaii's Spam Cookbook*.

- 1 (12-ounce) jar commercial kimchi (available at Asian markets)
- 1 (12-ounce) can Spam luncheon meat, sliced in 1/2-inch slivers
- 1 small onion, sliced
- 2 teaspoons soy sauce
- 1 medium zucchini, sliced (optional)
- 1 block firm tofu, sliced (optional)

Place kimchi in a strainer or colander and rinse with water. Drain well. Brown Spam slices in skillet. Add kimchi, onion, soy sauce, and, if desired, zucchini and tofu. Cook for about 2 minutes.

market still in place today. At least that's what the U.S. Army surmises from the fact that its Korean PXs sell 447,000 pounds of Spam a year to only 60,000 authorized customers. That's 7.45 pounds of Spam a year per authorized person—or only a little less than the annual per capita consumption of chocolate in the United States. Although Hormel Foods has licensed the local Cheil Foods company to make and sell Spam in Korea, Spam is so much cheaper in the PXs that black marketers can take a hefty markup and still offer Korean consumers bootleg Spam at bargain-basement prices. A similar problem with American beer has caused U.S. military officials to set quotas on beer

Spam cans from (left to right) Korea (Smoke Flavored), Australia, French Canada, and Korea (regular).

purchases by U.S. soldiers. Officials apparently don't have the nerve to try to set similar limits on Spam sales.

There is also a substantial "gray market" of Spam shipped into Korea from U.S. supermarket warehouses without the permission of Hormel Foods. The company's Crane reports frequent calls from Korean American entrepreneurs interested in picking up a shipping container or two of Spam. When he explains that this is not the way Hormel Foods does business, they say, "I won't tell anyone." And when he still refuses, they say, "Does your boss know you are turning me down?"

Since South Korea opened up to foreign food importers in 1987, there have been fewer brands of soy sauce on Korean supermarket shelves than choices of luncheon meat. They include 25% Less Salt Spam, Spam Smoke Flavored, and Spam with Cheese Chunks; cut-priced European brands such as Plumrose, Dak, and Tulip; and the locally produced knockoff Lo-Spam.

But only American Spam has the cachet to be considered gourmet. In fact, almost half of all Korean Spam sales occur during that country's autumn Harvest Moon Festival gift-giving season. Go into the gift section of Seoul's toniest department stores then and you'll find presentation boxes and briefcases full of Spam priced at $35 to $75 right beside Swiss chocolates and bottles of wine. Individual cans go for about $3 each. (Since Korean salaries are about half those in the United States, that's equivalent to about $6.) That could explain why per capita consumption is a modest eighth of a pound—compared to Guam's eight pounds.

Guam: SPAM Capital of the World

As a U.S. territory, Guam gets no voting rights but complete access to Spam. That privilege started with World War II and continues largely because of the

This Korean Spam gift box comes complete with oil for frying.

influence of the U.S. military base. There's another important reason, though, that Chamorros (Guam natives) call Spam Chamorro steak and consume more of it than any other people on the planet: Guam suffers frequent typhoons that leave residents without power for weeks on end.

Even when the power's on, the local Shirley's restaurant chain goes through twelve dozen cans of Spam a day making the popular breakfast of Spam, eggs, and fried rice—a dish that reportedly is served regularly at Government House, the Guamanian equivalent of the White House. Moreover, Spam sails off of chest-high end-of-aisle supermarket displays in Guam at a rate of up to 350 cans a day. A Toyota dealer on the island has even used it as a sales come-on—offering to fill the trunk of every new car with Spam. And Dorothy Horn, author and self-publisher of two Spam cookbooks, is the most famous and well-respected food critic on the island.

The Queen of SPAManian Cuisine

Almost all of the Spam recipe books put out by Hormel Foods contain at least some international recipes. But the company's accomplishments on that front don't begin to compare with those of Dorothy Horn, who developed five hundred Spam recipes based on the cuisines of fifty different cultures—from Australia to Yap Island—and published them all in a book entitled *Great Classic Spam Recipes of the World*. Horn says she was inspired to take up the global Spam challenge by the island's many foreign influences. (Guam was once settled by Spain and the Philippines and today receives many visitors from Japan and Korea.)

Dorothy Horn
Cookbook Author

Horn claims to have tasted every one of her recipes, including Home Made Spam and Snake Soup from Hong Kong, which "yields four servings—more if you let the guests know what is in it before you serve it." Some recipes she tried out with friends at her home. ("The really good friends I've seen again," she says.) Others she served at an elegant 1994 cocktail party attended by the Guam governor at which she also used flowers carved from Spam to adorn her fruit trays. A highlight of CNN's coverage of the event was an interview with Hormel Foods employee Peter Hoeper, who compared Spam to music in the way that it inspires creativity. It certainly has inspired Horn.

SPAMming the Pacific

Spam is almost as popular on the nearby Solomon, Caroline, and Marshall islands. In his book *The Happy Isles of Oceania*, travel writer Paul Theroux theorizes that "former cannibals of Oceania" now feast on Spam because it comes "the nearest to approximating the porky taste of human flesh." Who knows, perhaps he's right.

SPAM Kelaguen

In her first Spam cookbook, *Guam's Winning Gourmet Spam Lite Luncheon Meat Recipes from Dorothy's Kitchen,* Dorothy Horn combined award-winning recipes from a local department store's annual Spam cook-off with her own Spam interpretations of such Guamanian staples as this one, a marinated meat dish.

- 1 (12-ounce) can Spam Lite luncheon meat, mashed
- 2 tablespoons fresh lemon juice
- 1/2 medium onion, diced
- 2 green onions, chopped
- 1 1/2 tablespoons grated fresh coconut
- Salt to taste
- Red pepper to taste

Combine all ingredients in a large bowl and chill thoroughly before serving on tortillas or crackers.

Spam is, after all, made from pig, and Polynesians have long called human meat "long pig."

The U.S. military has played a Spam role on other Pacific islands as well. Take the tiny country of Palau, for instance, which was the site of one of the bloodiest battles of World War II. Today, generous U.S. aid, prompted by fears that a major power will once again try to take over its tiny

SPAMless in Taiwan

With its history of U.S. military involvement, its warm climate, and its pork-loving population, Taiwan perfectly fits Hormel Foods' profile of a foreign country with the potential for big Spam sales. Yet the company has twice tried and failed to sell Spam in Taiwan: once by exporting U.S.-made product, the other time by licensing the rights to a local food company. Richard Crane, director of marketing and sales for Hormel Foods International, speculates that the ready supply of fresh pork in Taiwan, the people's competing love for fish, and their unfamiliarity with canned meats could all have played a role in the failure. Even so, he says, "I'm still surprised we didn't do better."

but strategic airstrip, has produced a welfare nation. Natives who used to fish or farm for their food now live on a food-stamp-purchased diet of convenience foods, sweets, Spam, and other canned meats, which local physicians blame for increasing rates of heart disease and diabetes. These complaints are echoed by neurologist-author Oliver Sacks in *The Island of the Colorblind,* a 1997 account of his trip to Micronesia.

Spam sales are just moderate in Japan proper but go gangbusters on Okinawa, where more than twenty-six thousand U.S. troops are stationed. Okinawans eat an average of 1.7 pounds of Spam a person annually, which puts them behind only Guamanians and Hawaiians in per capita consumption. Yet Okinawan women are among the world's longest living. (Dr. Sacks should write an article explaining *that.*)

The Late, Great SPAMland

Once the kings and queens of Spam sales outside the United States, British subjects now eat slightly less Spam than the Yanks who rebelled against them, and the downward trend in consumption appears likely to continue. Spam commands only about 30 percent of the luncheon meat market in the United Kingdom, versus 60 percent in the United States, and sales of all canned meats there are diving at a rate of about 6 percent a year.

Why? In addition to lend-lease overkill during World War II, England had ten years to get sick of Spam afterwards as part of postwar rationing programs. These programs helped to inspire the devastating Monty Python Spam skit, another factor. And marketing materials by longtime British Spam licensee Newforge Foods didn't help. While everyone else was talking about nutrition in terms of fat and calories, Newforge was still rhapsodizing about the miracle of canning, then three hundred years old, and boasting of Spam's vitamin content. Although this probably wasn't the reason, Tulip International of Denmark now makes all British Spam for Hormel Foods.

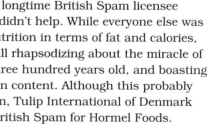

Learning to Speak SPAMmish

"**S**pam speaks any language—and with such sparkle!" enthuses Margaret Fulton in the "Spam International Cookbook" supplement to the May 11, 1970, issue of *Woman's Day.* You may not be quite as linguistically versatile, but before you take off on your next world tour, you should bone up on some of the dialects of Spammish spoken in other countries.

ENGLAND: Spam here may taste a bit different because it's made from pork and rind rather than the rindless ham used in the States. It's referred to as "chopped pork and ham" and comes in rectangular as well as round cans, which are about twice as popular,

with the labels on both picturing Spam accompanied by lettuce and tomato. In addition, Brits can select packages of presliced round or wafer-thin Spam, or they can get Spam sliced to order from big round loaves at the deli. They can also choose Spam Spreaders, ground Spam products similar to American Spam Spread except that they come in four flavors: original (plain), with pineapple, with onion and chives, and smoked.

In 1987, then Spam licensee Newforge Foods tried out Spam and Tongue, but the Brits did not bite. They didn't swallow a frozen pizza topped with creamy white cheese and triangular wedges of Spam, either, even though they had made a runaway success of one topped with Heinz baked beans. The newest Spam offering in the United Kingdom is Spam Premium Flakes of Ham, a product similar to American canned chunk ham.

THE PHILIPPINES: Called Agojo Spam after producing licensee Agojo & Sons, the luncheon meat is sold in the Philippines in a round can adorned with a light blue label featuring cartoonish drawings. Ingredients include the familiar pork, salt, sugar, and water as well as the more mysterious fos-fat, praque powder, and California spice.

JAPAN: Japanese Spam comes in a rectangular can about a third the size of the American one. The 25-percent-less-sodium variety sells so well that in 1997 a 40-percent-less-sodium version was introduced.

KOREA: Hormel discontinued Spam with Cheese Chunks in the United States some years back, but regular and reduced-salt versions of both it and Spam Smoke Flavored are sold in Korea. Almost 98 percent of Korean Spam sales are of reduced-salt products. Despite their famed love for garlic, Koreans did not take to a garlic-flavored Spam when it was offered. The biggest difference between Spam here and in the United States is its lack of gelatin. Koreans so dislike gelatin that Spam licensee Cheil Foods adds starch to absorb it.

Spam is exported to the other forty-six foreign countries where it is sold and so in most of those places looks and tastes the same way that it does in the United States. Two exceptions are Canada, where one side of the Spam Lite can reads "Spam Léger" (in deference to French- speaking residents of Quebec province), and Australia, where Spam is called Spam Spiced Ham and Spam Smoke Flavored has a red label instead of a brown one.

When Spam *is* purchased in England today, it's usually by working-class families who serve it in sandwiches or as fritters, which they can also buy ready-to-eat at some fish-and-chips shops. To appeal to this audience, British Spam ads appear in women's tabloids alongside such stories as "The Ultimate Betrayal: 'My husband ran off with my mum'" and "They said I was too sexy for my job."

In one of the ads in the early '90s, an overwhelmed mum confesses, "Tea-time was looking nasty, the kids were hungry, they wanted food, and fast!" Then in a flash of the Batman-style action words—"Wham! Bam! Thank you, Spam!"—she thinks of serving a Spamburger hamburger. In a more recent ad, a hyperactive "Spam-mad" kid recites a rap poem about the many ways he enjoys Spam: "You can eat it in a sandwich, you can eat it off a plate. You can eat it in a salad, you can eat it with a mate."

Classical music lent a touch of class to British Spam TV ads in the '60s.

SPAM Fritters

This recipe for Spam fritters, a favorite in England, comes from a recipe poster produced by former British Spam licensee Newforge Foods.

    3/4 cup flour
    Pinch of salt
    1 egg, separated
    1/2 cup milk
    1 (12-ounce) can Spam
        luncheon meat
    Oil for frying
    Barbecue sauce

Sift flour and salt together and then beat in egg yolk and milk until smooth. Dice Spam and add to batter. Whisk egg white until stiff and fold into batter. Drop spoonfuls of batter into deep, hot oil. Cook until golden and crisp, approximately 3 to 4 minutes. Drain. Serve immediately on cocktail sticks with your favorite barbecue sauce. Serves 6.

Both ads contrast dramatically with British TV commercials for Spam in the '60s, which featured opera and classical choral groups. Of course those were also the days when a Spam-sponsored powerboat race attracted royalty in the person of Prince Philip.

From Anguilla to Zimbabwe

Elsewhere around the globe, Hormel Foods has had some success selling Spam in the ex–British colonies of Australia and Canada, it has three promising new markets—Mexico, Poland, and China—and it's been keeping tabs on the political changes in the former Soviet Union, a lend-lease recipient of Spam during World War II. Former Hormel

Princesses and swamis had starring roles in these Spanish-language cartoon ads from the 1960s.

President Richard Knowlton presented cans of Spam to both Mikhail Gorbachev and his successor, Boris Yeltsin, on their visits to the U.S. Midwest in 1990 and 1992, respectively. In fact, all told, Spam luncheon meat is trademarked in more than a hundred countries—from Anguilla to Zimbabwe—and is sold in fifty of them.

So where in the world can a person be safe from Spam? Only in the Middle East, where Islamic bans on pork make trying to sell it a really bad idea.

THERE'S A WORLD OF THINGS YOU CAN DO WITH SPAM.

GOOD FOOD FOR THE WORLD
SPAM

SPAM para PLATOS SABROSOS

SPAM Around the Globe

Starring SPAM

It's one thing when chefs and cookbook authors talk about a foodstuff, quite another when the food is featured in movies, TV shows, novels, poetry, artwork, and the theater. The former is to be expected if the food is going to be successful; the latter happens only to the handful of products that have become so much a part of the fabric of our culture that they linger in the minds of creative people long after they've been digested. Such is the case with Spam luncheon meat.

The "miracle meat" long ago earned a place in our cupboards. What follows

The Instant Monty Python CD Collection

is a survey of some of the ways it has acted, sung, juggled, written, drawn, painted, rhymed, and generally entertained its way into our hearts.

SPAM on the Tube

SPAM, SPAM, SPAM, PYTHON AND SPAM The most famous of all media references to Spam is undoubtedly the closing skit of the December 15, 1970, episode of the BBC comedy series *Monty Python's Flying Circus*. In it a couple literally drops (on wires) into a café where almost everything on the menu contains Spam. This is a source of dismay to the wife, who says she doesn't like Spam, but an apparent delight to the group of Vikings at a neighboring table, who start singing about Spam with gusto.

The years this sketch first began airing on public television stations in the United States were defining ones in the history of Spam. Before 1974, Spam was a source of humor mainly to World War II veterans and their loved ones. After this sketch became widely known, it was hard for anyone to think about Spam seriously again.

The skit became a signature piece of Python surrealism—so much so that when the English Academy of Film and Television held a twenty-fifth anniversary Monty Python party in 1994, Spam was on the menu. Spam also shows up regularly at refreshment stands in movie theaters holding Python film festivals, and it is the name of the official Python cyberspace fan club.

Despite the notoriety of the Spam sketch, very little has been said or printed about its genesis. Since all but one of the Pythons grew up in England during World War II, they presumably were as overwhelmed by lend-lease shipments of Spam as everyone else in the country. Since Pythons Terry Jones and Michael Palin share writing credits for the Spam song in the skit, the two of them presumably wrote the rest of the piece as well. "I don't think we ever got permission from the [Hormel] company. We just went ahead," Palin once told the *Independent* of London. "In the end the Spam people were very keen and promised to send us several tins of free Spam. We said, 'No, that's all right. Thanks anyway.'"

Beyond that, all we know is what Python expert Kim "Howard" Johnson did not find in the rehearsal script for the now classic episode—this Spam skit:

Setting: A cafe where all the customers are VIKINGS

Enter MR. AND MRS. BUN *downwards (on wires)*

MR. BUN [Eric Idle]. Morning.
WAITRESS [Terry Jones]. Morning.
MR. BUN. What have you got, then?
WAITRESS. Well, there's egg and bacon; egg, sausage, and bacon; egg and Spam; egg, bacon, and Spam; egg, bacon, sausage, and Spam; Spam, bacon, sausage, and Spam; Spam, egg, Spam, Spam, bacon, and Spam; Spam, Spam, Spam, egg, and Spam; Spam, Spam, Spam, Spam, Spam, Spam, baked beans, Spam, Spam, Spam, and Spam; or lobster thermidor aux crevettes with a Mornay sauce garnished with truffle pâté, brandy, and a fried egg on top and Spam.
MRS. BUN [Graham Chapman]. Have you got anything without Spam in it?

WAITRESS. Well, Spam, egg, sausage, and Spam. That's not got *much* Spam in it.

MRS. BUN. I don't want *any* Spam.

MR. BUN. Why can't she have egg, bacon, Spam, and sausage?

MRS. BUN. That's got Spam in it!

MR. BUN. Not as much as Spam, egg, sausage, and Spam.

MRS. BUN. Look, could I have egg, bacon, Spam, and sausage without the Spam?

WAITRESS. Uuuuuuggggh!

MRS. BUN. What d'you mean, uuugggh? I don't like Spam!

VIKINGS. [*singing*] Spam, Spam, Spam, Spam. Spam, Spam, Spam, Spam. Lovely Spam, wonderful Spam. [*Brief stock shot of a Viking ship.*] Lovely Spam, wonderful Spam . . .

WAITRESS. Shut up! Shut up! Shut up! You can't have egg, bacon, Spam, and sausage without the Spam.

MRS. BUN. Why not?

WAITRESS. No, it wouldn't be egg, bacon, Spam, and sausage, would it?

MRS. BUN. I don't like Spam!

MR. BUN. Don't make a fuss, dear. I'll have your Spam. I love it. I'm having Spam, Spam, Spam, Spam, Spam, Spam . . .

VIKINGS. [*singing*] Spam, Spam, Spam, Spam . . .

MR. BUN. . . . Spam, baked beans, Spam, Spam, and Spam.

WAITRESS. Baked beans are off.

MR. BUN. Well, can I have Spam instead?

WAITRESS. You mean Spam, Spam, Spam, Spam, Spam, Spam, Spam, Spam, Spam . . .

VIKINGS. [*still singing*] Spam, Spam, Spam, Spam . . .

MR. BUN. Yes.

WAITRESS. Arrggh!

VIKINGS. . . . Lovely Spam, wonderful Spam . . .

WAITRESS. Shut up! Shut up!

[*The* VIKINGS *shut up momentarily. Enter the* HUNGARIAN (*from an earlier sketch*).]

HUNGARIAN [John Cleese]. Great boobies, honeybun. My lower intestine is full of Spam, egg, Spam, bacon, Spam, tomato, Spam . . .

VIKINGS. [*starting up again*] Spam, Spam, Spam, Spam . . . [*etc.*]

WAITRESS. Shut up! Shut up!

[*A policeman rushes in and bundles the* HUNGARIAN *out.*]

HUNGARIAN. My nipples explode . . .

[*Cut to a* HISTORIAN. *Superimposed caption:* A Historian.]

HISTORIAN [Michael Palin]. Another great Viking victory was at the Green Midget café in Bromley. Once again the Viking strategy was the same. They sailed from these fjords here [*indicating a map with arrows on it*], assembled at Trondheim, and waited for the strong northeasterly winds to blow their oaken galleys to England, whence they sailed on May the twenty-third. Once in Bromley they assembled in the Green Midget café and Spam selecting a Spam particular Spam item from the Spam menu would Spam, Spam, Spam, Spam . . .

[*The backdrop behind the* HISTORIAN *rises to reveal the café again. The* VIKINGS *start singing again and the* HISTORIAN *conducts them.*]

VIKINGS. [*singing*] Spam, Spam, Spam, Spam. Spam, Spam, Spam, Spam. Lovely Spam, wonderful Spam. Lovely Spam, wonderful Spam . . .

[MR. AND MRS. BUN *rise slowly in the air. Superimposed caption:* In 1970 Monty Python's Flying Circus lay in ruins, and then the words on the screen said . . . The End. *Fade out and roll credits, which are sprinkled liberally with Spam, eggs, sausage, chips, and tomato—but especially Spam.*]

A party-hearty Colonel Blake (McLean Stevenson) raises a bottle to the Spam lamb on *M*A*S*H*.

SPAM LAMB The December 31, 1974, episode of the popular Korean War TV comedy *M*A*S*H* revolves around Radar (Gary Burghoff) and his new pet lamb. Finding out that his precious pet is due to be barbecued at a bash for some visiting Greek troops, Radar phonies up some medical discharge papers and gets plane passage to his parents' home for one Private Charles Lamb. To save Radar's neck and the Greek feast, Hawkeye (Alan Alda) and Trapper John (Wayne Rogers) stay up half the night sculpting the visual punch line of the episode: a lamb sculpted from Spam.

Lobster Thermidor aux Crevettes with a Mornay Sauce Garnished with Truffle Pâté, Brandy, and a Fried Egg on Top and SPAM

The late Louis Szathmary earned his culinary stripes at the famed Bakery restaurant in Chicago, where he was both owner and chef. Later in life he was named chef laureate of Johnson and Wales University. But his humbler beginnings included cooking with Spam luncheon meat competitor Treet as executive chef for the Armour meat company in the late '50s. Szathmary called on all of his culinary experience to develop this recipe for the fanciest dish on Monty Python's Green Midget café menu.

For the truffle pâté:

- 1 (2 1/2–3-ounce) can black truffles
- 1/2 cup semisweet sherry
- 1 cup imported pâté foie gras (goose liver pâté)
- 2 tablespoons sweet butter (at room temperature)
- 1–2 tablespoons brandy or cognac

For the lobster thermidor:

- 1 1 1/2-pound live lobster
- 1 tablespoon corn oil
- 1/2 teaspoon sea or kosher salt
- 1/2 cup lobster stock (or water)
- 1/2 cup white wine
- 1/2 cup canned consommé (or 1 tablespoon beef base diluted in 1/2 cup water or 1/2 cup canned beef gravy)
- Pinch of chervil
- Pinch of tarragon
- 1/2 tablespoon chopped shallots
- 1/2 cup condensed cream of chicken soup
- Pinch of dried English mustard
- 1/4 pound (1 stick) sweet butter

For the Mornay sauce:

- 6 ounces lobster roasting liquid (or bottled clam juice)
- 1 cup condensed cream of chicken soup
- 2 tablespoons light cream
- 1/2 cup grated Gruyère cheese
- 1/2 cup grated Parmesan cheese
- 1/2 stick sweet butter

For the finale:

- 2 tablespoons Parmesan cheese
- 2 eggs with enough butter to fry
- 1 (7-ounce) can Spam luncheon meat, sliced in half the long way
- 3 to 4 small shrimp, deveined and cooked

To make the truffle pâté: Strain the liquid from the canned truffles. Cut the truffles into small pieces and put them in a food processor with the sherry and canned or other type of prepared goose liver pâté. Add half the butter and brandy. Mix. Add the rest of the butter and brandy. Mix again. Cover and chill until serving time.

To make the lobster thermidor: Preheat oven to 450 degrees. Split the live lobster in half lengthwise, inserting a very sharp knife where the body and tail armor meet. Remove and discard the "stomach" (the greenish bag in the middle of the armor). Remove the legs and claws, and pick out all the meat from them and the body, leaving the body shell intact. Dice larger pieces of meat into 1/2- to 3/4-inch pieces. Rinse the two empty lobster shells under running water, brush slightly with oil, and place in a roasting pan. Lightly salt the lobster meat and place it next to the shells in the pan. Pour a cup of water into the pan and put the pan in the oven for 20 minutes.

Remove the shells and place them on an ovenproof platter. Strain the liquid from the roasted lobster pieces. Make the thermidor sauce by combining the roasting juices (or water), white wine, consommé, chervil, tarragon, shallots, soup, mustard, and butter in a saucepan over low heat. Spoon some of the sauce into the shells. Fill the shells with the lobster meat and cover with the rest of the sauce. Refrigerate until just before serving time.

To make the Mornay sauce: Cook the roasting liquid (or clam juice), soup, and cream together in a small pan. Over medium heat reduce the sauce. Add the Gruyère and Parmesan cheese. Heat until the cheeses melt. Whisk the butter into the sauce. Keep hot until serving time.

To complete the extravaganza: Set the oven to 400 degrees. Heat the lobster platter through, not longer than 5 minutes. Sprinkle 2 tablespoons Parmesan cheese on top and put under the broiler for 1 minute to get some color. Spoon the Mornay sauce on top.

Meanwhile, fry two eggs in a little butter on medium heat. Fry or grill the slices of Spam. Serve the Spam and the fried egg on top of the Mornay-topped lobster and garnish with some of the truffle pâté and shrimp. Serve with French bread and boiled fresh asparagus, if desired. Serves 2.

Demonstrating the versatility of "the Hormel meat of many uses," Jay Leno slicks back his hair with Spam gel and builds a Spam dike.

extract bread spread from Down Under (in conjunction with a guest appearance by Australian model Elle MacPherson); a Super Bowl 1996 conversation with Tom Arnold about a wacky sporting event at which Spam was the prize; a spring 1996 sketch in which Leno slid out of the Spam NASCAR racing car with the aid of his gelatin coating; and an April 1998 segment in which he helped Alberta Dunbar make her prize-winning Spam cheesecake (mainly by spiking it with lots of cognac).

And that's just in the past several years. Not long after Leno first took over *The Tonight Show*, he hit the streets of Los Angeles to get feedback on Spang, a refresher he created by blending Spam and Tang. And one 1992 monologue included the following joke: "Now they've come out with a new low-calorie Spam, called Spam Lite. But let me tell you, if you're eating Spam on a regular basis, I don't think calories are your biggest problem."

JOKING JAY One of the most noticeable changes in *The Tonight Show* since Jay Leno took over has been the increase in Spam jokes and sketches. They have included a March 1995 skit demonstrating alternatives to eating Spam; a May 1995 face-off between Spam and Vegemite, a yeast-

SECRET INGREDIENT Spam has had a recurring role in NBC-TV's suspense series *The Pretender* ever since a 1997 episode in which hero Jarod Russell poses as a federal marshal. In that episode Russell gets his first taste of Spam in the squad room at lunchtime and declares it "delicious." Later, he

And Now, He-r-e's SPAM Cheesecake!

For this recipe for Savory International Spam Cheesecake, Alberta Dunbar won more than just the grand prize in the 1997 National Best Spam Recipe Contest—a $2,500 shopping spree at the Mall of America in Minneapolis. She also landed an appearance on *The Tonight Show*.

Crust:
- 3/4 cup seasoned bread crumbs
- 1/4 cup ground toasted almonds or pine nuts
- 1/4 teaspoon ground nutmeg
- 1/4 cup melted butter

Filling:
- 2 (8-ounce) containers garden-vegetable-flavored cream cheese
- 3 eggs
- 1/2 cup crumbled tomato-basil-flavored feta cheese
- 1/2 cup crumbled blue cheese
- 1/4 cup chopped black olives
- 1 tablespoon all-purpose flour
- 1 teaspoon Italian seasoning
- 1 tablespoon brandy (or 1/2 teaspoon brandy extract)
- 1 (12-ounce) can Spam luncheon meat, grated

Topping:
- 1 cup sour cream
- 2 teaspoons sugar
- 1 (10-ounce) jar Patak's Major Grey chutney, pureed
- 1/3 cup toasted slivered almonds or pine nuts

Preheat oven to 350 degrees. In small bowl, combine all crust ingredients. Gently press into bottom of 10-inch springform pan or pie plate. Bake 8 to 10 minutes. Set aside to cool. Reduce oven temperature to 300 degrees.

In large bowl, beat cream cheese until light and fluffy. Add eggs, one at a time, beating well after each addition. Stir in next six filling ingredients. Gently fold in Spam. Pour into prepared crust and bake 50 to 60 minutes or until center is almost set.

In small bowl combine sour cream and sugar. Spread over cheesecake and bake 10 additional minutes. Cool to room temperature. Refrigerate several hours or overnight. Before serving, spread chutney over cheescake and sprinkle toasted nuts around outside edge. Cut into thin wedges and serve with assorted crackers. Serves 24.

Jay Leno with Alberta Dunbar.

sculpts a caseload of Spam into the torso of an AWOL informant and uses it to figure out how he escaped. The episode ends at a Texas cook-off with Russell dishing out samples of a chili whose secret ingredient is you-know-what.

There's nothing fake about the TV Pretender's love for Spam.

TV Dinner

Pretend to be the TV Pretender and whip up a big pot of Spam chili. This recipe is from *Great Classic Spam Recipes of the World* by Dorothy Horn.

2 (12-ounce) cans Spam luncheon meat, ground
1/2 cup onions, chopped
4 garlic cloves, minced
4 cups water
4 tablespoons chili powder
4 tablespoons flour
2 (16-ounce) cans kidney beans
1 (16-ounce) can tomatoes
1 (4-ounce) can tomato sauce
1 ounce dark chocolate, melted

Lightly brown Spam in skillet with onions and garlic. Add remaining ingredients and simmer for 20 to 30 minutes. Serve in bowls with chopped onion, if desired, and crackers. Serves 4 to 6.

SPAM on the Big Screen

THANK YOU, WHAM The 1948 film *Mr. Blandings Builds His Dream House* is about a fixer-upper purchased by advertising executive Jim Blandings (Cary Grant) and his wife, Muriel (Myrna Loy). Blandings' agency's big account and therefore the source of much of the money the couple are pouring into their house is Wham, a meat that looks like ham and so clearly refers to Spam that a Hormel company newsletter of the era contained this verse:

Spam is the name
Of the new Hormel dish.
Wham grows its fame
Is the Hormel wish.

The movie's climax shows Blandings desperately trying to devise a new advertising campaign that will save the Wham account and, by extension, his house. After staying at the office all night and coming up empty, a defeated Blandings returns home, and his beaming maid Gussie (Louise Beavers) hands him the catchy slogan he's been looking for. As she serves him Wham and eggs for breakfast, she declares, "If you ain't eatin' Wham, you ain't eatin' ham."

STINGO'S CHOICE Spam provides one of the only comic moments in the movie version of William Styron's Holocaust novel, *Sophie's Choice*. Right near the beginning of the film, Stingo (Peter MacNicol), preparing to hole up and write the Great American Novel, staggers into a room he has just rented with a few cases of Spam on his shoulder.

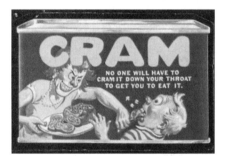

Cram stickers were part of the Wacky Package school notebook decorating craze of the 1970s.

The Spam teeters there precariously for a minute and then spills all over the floor.

DISASTER DINNER Kevin Costner's 1995 film *Waterworld*, a box office megaflop, offers a grim vision of a future after environmental apocalypse, especially for the survivors who end up slaves aboard a rusty freighter ruled over by the evil Deacon

(Dennis Hopper). When Deacon, standing on an upper deck, empties sacks of canned meat onto his crowd of hungry charges, a close-up of the Spam clone Smeat telegraphs just how starving these people must be.

SPAM on Stage

Jack Swersie is a comic juggler and his medium is Spam, in and out of the can. He has juggled Spam at

Hormel Foods Corporation v. Kermit the Frog

A wild boar puppet named Spa'am has less than five minutes of screen time in *Muppet Treasure Island*, a movie that might have amused a few five-year-olds and then retreated quietly to the video racks had Hormel Foods Corporation not decided to sue. In this Jim Henson Productions spin on the Robert Louis Stevenson pirate tale, Spa'am is the high priest of a tribe of wild boars that live on Treasure Island and worship Miss Piggy, whom they call their Queen Boom Sha-Ka-La-Ka-La. Wearing a headdress of a human skull and a necklace of small pig heads, Spa'am sentences Kermit and several other lovable, fuzzy Muppets to death before joining with them against the even more

threatening Long John Silver (Tim Curry).

In a trademark infringement suit filed in a Manhattan federal court in July 1995, Hormel Foods attorneys called the Spa'am character "evil in porcine form" and said they feared the name, because of its obvious similarity to *Spam,* might make the public lose its hunger for their meat product. With court decisions on the books that had stopped a comic from calling himself Kodak and a designer from selling Mutant of Omaha clothing, they believed they had a good case against *Muppet Treasure Island*.

But the legal issues were for the most part dwarfed by the media circus that erupted around the case, in part because the federal judge assigned to it, an ex–Playboy bunny and one-time Clinton nominee for U.S. attorney general, was embroiled in an affair with a married millionaire whose mushy diary entries about her had just hit the tabloids.

Hormel Foods lost the case and its appeal. In upholding Judge Kimba Wood, the appeals court noted that "countless jokes have played off the public's unfounded suspicion that Spam is a product of less than savory

ingredients." If anything, the judges said, the company should be grateful to have the product associated with a "genuine source of pork."

What SPAM and Kleenex Have in Common

Muppet Treasure Island was the most widely publicized case of Hormel Foods coming to the legal defense of its best-known trademark, but it is hardly the only one. Trademark names and their associations are such valuable assets that companies live in mortal fear of their generification. So if Hormel Foods lawyers seem excessively zealous, it's only because they want to avoid future crying in their Kleenex over people Xeroxing the company's luncheon meat.

Set Dressing

You might assume that Spam appears in a movie or television show because of the love a writer or director or character has for the product. But sometimes it's simply paid advertising, otherwise known as product placement. Since 1986, when Hormel retained a Hollywood firm to secure cameo appearances for its products, Spam has shown up on the shelves in kitchens or stores on such popular television shows as *Northern Exposure, Mad about You,* and *The Larry Sanders Show.* It has also had bit parts in at least three movies: *Empire of the Sun,* in which it rains down with other Red Cross air relief supplies on the starving young English hero and is, in fact, the first thing the boy lunges at; *Grumpy Old Men,* in which widower Jack Lemmon slices himself a Spam dinner in a small Minnesota town not far from Spam headquarters; and *Blankman,* in which the eponymous superhero (Damon Wayans) wears a can of Spam on his belt of brand-name crime-fighting gadgets (but never demonstrates its exact purpose).

Jack Swersie juggles Spam on *Music City Tonight.*

Harrah's and Caesars Palace, on TNN's *Music City Tonight,* and as an opening act for Perry Como, Melissa Manchester, the Oak Ridge Boys, Dionne Warwick, and Harry Blackstone Jr.

Swersie started juggling Spam in the can around 1990 as a substitute for a Rubik's Cube in a routine also involving a machete and an apple. "The Rubik's Cube was getting dated, and I wanted to replace it with something that seemed funny," he explained.

Swersie started juggling Spam out of the can in 1994, and that's even funnier. His signature routine involves a lit cigar, a top hat, and a block of Spam Lite, which he takes a bite out of in midflight—a dramatic moment that almost always elicits a gasp from the audience. When the routine ends, Swersie has the cigar in his mouth and the Spam on his head, with the top hat on top of that. (Yes, he does use an oily hair shampoo.) Why Spam Lite? Swersie says it's not as slippery as regular, so it's easier to juggle.

Swersie's latest Spam routine, which he's performed on television several times, is a midair taste test of regular Spam, Spam Lite, and Spam Smoke

Flavored in which he juggles and discusses the virtues of the products between bites. His publicity materials note that he is "ready to book with no refrigeration necessary."

Other SPAM Sightings

❑ In *The Right Stuff*, the 1983 movie adaptation of Tom Wolfe's novel about the early days of the Mercury space program, Sam Shepard (playing the part of test pilot Chuck Yeager) warns that anyone who agrees to climb on top of one of the rockets "is going to be Spam in a can."

❑ On his late show one night in 1987, David Letterman introduced America to an innovative new product: Spam-on-a-rope—for people "who are really on the go and who like to eat in the shower."

❑ A recording of a 1994 Grateful Dead concert called *Dick's Picks Volume 7* includes the tasty "Spam Jam," a segue of "instrumental, atonal strangeness" that, according to Dead publicist Dennis McNally, got its name as "a joke" because the CD's producers, who had to call it something for legal purposes, liked "the way it rhymes."

❑ In John Welter's 1994 comic novel *Night of the Avenging Blowfish,* a White House chef is fired for serving Spam at a state dinner, and a scandal erupts over the president's apparent disdain for foods of the common man.

❑ In a 1997 episode of the television situation comedy *Frasier*, Sherry offers to make a flu-wracked Frasier a breakfast of scrambled egg tacos and Spam patties. He quips under his breath, "In keeping with the trusty adage 'Starve a cold, disgust a fever'?"

SPAM in Song, Art, and Fashion

STANDING BY HIS SPAM In 1989 rock-and-roll song parodist Weird Al Yankovic made his first feature-length film, *UHF*. That has nothing to do with Spam, but "Spam" was one of several songs added to Yankovic's simultaneously released album, *UHF: Original Motion Picture Soundtrack and Other Stuff.* The R.E.M. "Stand" takeoff also appears on 1993's

The Food Album, a smorgasbord of previously released Weird Al food fare.

In "Spam," Weird Al proclaims what "a darn good sandwich" this "mystery meat" makes (as well as "spackle or bathroom grout"), wonders "what's inside it," and enumerates some of the many places where a Spam junkie might want to stash it, including the back of the car. Before concluding with a wistful "Oh Spam,"

had Spam in the title. "Spam Again," which appears on the ex–Velvet Underground member's solo album *Life in Exile after Abdication*, is about her career as a Wal-Mart clerk, a job she took up in desperation after both VU and her marriage dissolved.

Weird Al declares that "Spam anyplace that you are" is "the best." He also offers these two tidbits of advice:

If you're running low, go to the store.
Carry some money, to help you buy more.
The tab is there, to open the can.
The can is there, to hold in the Spam.

. . . .

Now once you start in, you can't put it down.
Don't leave it sitting, or it'll turn brown.
The key is going, to open the tin.
The tin is there, to keep the Spam in.

LABORER'S LUNCH One of the first songs ever written by legendary punk rock drummer Moe Tucker

Moe Tucker ate a lot of Spam while working at this Wal-Mart.

The song, in calypsolike rhythms, rails against the inequities that exist between the owner and the workers in such a business. Though "very, very rich," the owner wants "more, more, more" and so refuses to give his workers "a raise or a benefit." As a result, he gets "richer for sure" while the workers "stay so poor." In the following verse from the song, Tucker uses Spam to symbolize the kind of food the workers can afford:

I'm goin' to work
Little baby, baby
I'm goin' to work
Today.
Mama's going to make
A dollar, dollar
And buy some Spam
Today.

SAVE (FERRIS) ON SPAM According to Southern California ska-punk-pop band Save Ferris, Spam not only is a favorite of Bruce Jenner but is also better than anything made by Oscar Mayer. In the chorus of its "Spam" song, the band sings exuberantly and imaginatively of the luncheon meat:

Spam
It's pink and it's oval
Spam
I buy it at the Mobil
Spam
It's made in Chernobyl
Spam

ARTIST'S INSPIRATION Los Angeles–based pop artist Edward Ruscha has worked with Pepto-Bismol and baked beans as well as more traditional mediums, has made a film about a man who seduces a woman in a giant bed made out of lettuce, and has published books full of snapshots of empty parking lots and buildings with for-sale signs in front of them. So it may not be surprising that Spam is the subject of one of his paintings.

"It was only the can and not the contents that inspired me," Ruscha insists of the painting, which hangs in the Los Angeles County Museum of Art. "The

This may look like an Ansel Adams shot of Yosemite Valley, but it's actually an award-winning photograph James Soe Nyun took of blocks of Spam and tofu he carved to look like Adams' circa 1972 "El Capitan and Half Dome, Clearing Thunderstorm." The photograph is part of Soe Nyun's Engineered Food Series, which explores the relationship between technology and the natural world. In this case, the San Diego photographer was also trying to explore the relationship between Spam and tofu. "Tofu is considered natural and healthy, and to many people Spam is just the opposite of that," Soe Nyun says. "And yet tofu is also a manufactured material that has its own group of passionate detractors and fans."

word *Spam* . . . and the sausage-shaped letters I thought were beautiful together with that scary yellow." Called *Actual Size* because of the realistic dimensions of the Spam can on it, Ruscha's painting is one of several he did in the sixties featuring monosyllabic words with "punch, power, and noise. To me the word *Spam* is similar to the sound of a bomb. So you have this noisy thing at the top and then this projectile flying after the noise, arcing across the sky like a shooting star."

Ruscha's works command six figures and praise from critics like *Newsweek*'s Mark Stevens, who has said that Ruscha's word paintings call "into question the relations between a word . . . and its look, its meaning and its context." Ruscha denies any such serious intentions for *Spam*. "It's an innocently beautiful little object," he says.

SPAM IN STYLE Cynthia Rowley is almost as well known for her sense of humor as for her sense of style. A New York fashion designer who uses her father as a model and rides to work on a motorcycle, Rowley made a Spam belt the signature piece of her spring 1995 fashion show and still won the prestigious Perry Ellis Award for New Fashion Talent that year. "I make realistic clothes for real people," she says, and a Spam belt was one way of "conceptually hitting people over the head with that idea."

Why Spam as *the* symbol of real people? In part because of a trip Rowley took in 1994 to China and Tibet, where there was nothing to eat but rice and yak (ox) for three weeks. Then "one day a Tibetan pulled out a can of Spam. And I thought it was the most delicious thing I had eaten in my whole life," she recalls. In fact, it made her want to give Spam "a little plug." As it happened, the luncheon meat also fit in well with the Las Vegas–style American glamour theme of her 1995 show.

Rowley and her employees made the buckles for the Spam belts by cutting out the front panels of Spam cans, backing them with leather, then decorating the edges of the leather with rhinestones. While they labored, Rowley's staff ate Spam for breakfast, lunch, and dinner for weeks until "we finally got sick of it and put it in some Tupperware and tried to give it away to homeless people in the subway station," she confesses. "But even homeless people are leery of open food, especially if it's Spam." That's one reason Rowley now makes Spam belts only by special order (for forty-two dollars each). The other reason, she says, is that the shelf life of Spam fashion is much less than the shelf life of real Spam.

SPAM in Print

FUNNY-PAPER FODDER A popular subject for cartoons, Spam has inspired at least one *Bloom County*, a *Sylvia*, and three memorable *Far Sides*. But no cartoonist has reached for the canned meat quite as often as Jack Ohman. Although he produces

SHOE

his *Mixed Media* strip out of Portland, Oregon, Ohman hails from Minnesota, where "Spam love is genetic, or at least atmospheric," he explains. "Nothing better than Spam with some cloves and pineapple, a boyhood staple . . . that will wind up as a polyp in fifty years, but you only live once."

SOUTHERN-FRIED SPAM

Lewis Grizzard has been called "a Faulkner for just plain folks." Former Atlanta Mayor Andrew Young once said, "He makes an art of poor-white-trash culture." It's no wonder, then, that the late humorist once wrote a column about Spam. The wonder is that he was also able to work Doris Day and sex into the same piece. Surely there are some Freudian connections to be made here:

THE DUPLEX

It was my mother who first introduced me to Spam. I'm not certain exactly how old I was. Seven or eight. But it was certainly long before my first sexual experience. Before I finally had sex for the first time, I'd eaten enough Spam to fill the back seat of a '57 Chevy, where initial sexual experiences often occurred when you could pay 50 cents to go to a drive-in and ignore a Doris Day movie.

. . . I picked up a newspaper the other day and there was a story about Spam. . . . The most important paragraph in that story was the one that finally explained to me exactly what is Spam:

Chopped pork, pork shoulder, with ham meat added, salt, water, sugar and sodium nitrite.

So, there you have it. Spam unveiled. It's pig and sodium nitrite, which—I seem to remember from chemistry class—you can also find in jet fuel.

Suggested names for the Hubert H. Humphrey Metrodome (to get sponsor's money)

Pillsbury: POP-IN-FRESH METRODOME

General Mills: TWINKIEDOME

Hormel: SPAMDOME

3M: scotchdome

ED FISCHER
© 1995 Rochester Post-Bulletin
Distributed by Extra Newspaper Features

I need to end this with some sort of tie-in with Doris Day and sex, but I can't think of anything.

All that sodium nitrite in all that Spam I ate in my childhood may have permanently damaged a few of my brain cells.

NO SPAM FOR CLAMS In the mid-1980s, Janet Schulman, editor-in-chief of juvenile books at Random House, asked Theodore Geisel (a.k.a. Dr. Seuss) if he could come up with a new word to replace *Spam* in *The Tooth Book.* "It's such a World War II word that kids today don't have a clue!" Schulman argued. Geisel conceded the point but after a few days of working on it came up empty. So *Spam* it remains:

MixeD MediA BY JACK OHMAN

© 1997 Tribune Media Services, Inc. All Rights Reserved

PROGRAM GUIDE FOR THE SPAM CHANNEL...

7 AM. GOOD MORNING, SPAMERICA!
...HOW ARE YOU FOLKS THIS MORNING? IN THE PINK, I HOPE...

9 AM. FISHING WITH SPAM
THANKS, BUT NO...

NOON. THE SPAM MOVIE. "THE SPAMITYVILLE HORROR"
NOT THE PROCESSED CANNED MEAT EXPERIMENT!!!

3 PM. BUILDING WITH SPAM.
SPAM MAKES EXCELLENT BRICK WALLS, BUT THEY SMELL BAD AFTER A DAY OR TWO...

6 PM. THE SPAM EVENING NEWS.
GOOD EVENING! GOOD EVENING!

Spam was one of the targets of this *Spy* magazine cover piece in which several writers posing as White House aides tried to talk the makers of some of America's biggest brands into compromising the highest office in the land. The undercover writers told then Spam brand manager Jeffrey Grev that President Clinton's favorite sandwich was grilled Spam and melted Wisconsin cheddar and that the president might be willing to say so publicly—for a price.

Outlaw SPAM

Despite its celebrity status—or because of it—Spam has had several brushes with the law. In 1981 in Eugene, Oregon, it was the focus of a spat of spray-painted graffiti that was attributed to punk music vandals by everyone but Police Chief James Packard, who speculated that "some disgruntled Korean War veterans" might be responsible. A veteran himself, Packard had his fill of Spam while in the service and "to me," he said, "it's a dirty word."

In 1984 in Washington, D.C., the four-letter luncheon meat put a Maine family under suspicion of a capital offense when security guards working the metal detectors at the Capitol building mistook the can of Spam Verna Staples was carrying in her purse for a bomb. Several tense minutes passed before Staples was able to explain that the only blast she was planning was a picnic lunch with her husband and kids.

In June 1996, Spam was implicated in the theft of some exotic animals from a South Florida breeding farm. Although birds as well as monkeys were stolen, the monkeys apparently suffered the greater mistreatment: They were served nothing but Spam. The suspect was charged with cruelty to animals in addition to grand theft and dealing in stolen property.

Besides these incidents, there have been at least two big Spam heists. In 1990 in Guam, a tractor-trailer driver stole about ten thousand dollars' worth of the luncheon meat from a Safeway warehouse before being apprehended. In 1995, a second scamster from Georgia was caught trying to sell 1,198 cases of stolen Spam to a food wholesaler in North Carolina. When the luncheon meat was later recovered, Assistant U.S. Attorney Jim Harper described it as "without question . . . the largest Spam seizure in the history of the district."

On the other hand, Spam has also played an occasional role as a crime stopper. In December 1996, for example, Mary Ashford was working the checkout at the EZMart convenience store in Denison, Texas, when a bandit wearing a pair of women's pink panties struck her on the head in an attempt to rob the cash register. Although thrown off her feet momentarily, Ashford quickly recovered, grabbed some Spam cans from a nearby shelf, and threw them at the bandit, who fled without any money.

"Clams have no teeth,"
  says Pam the clam.
"I cannot eat
  hot dogs
  or ham."

"No teeth at all,"
  says Pam the clam.
"I cannot eat
  roast leg of lamb.
  Or peanuts! Pizzas!
  Popcorn! SPAM!
  Not even huckleberry jam!"

S itting on your
P late,
A
M ysterious stranger

S ir, as President of
   Hormel, you have
   been convicted by a
   jury of your
P eers on a charge of
"A ttempted
M eat."

S omehow the texture, out of nowhere
P roduces a species
A tavistic anomie, a
M elancholy memory of "food."

THE SPAM POETRY FLAP Spam has inspired much poetry, as anyone who has cruised Spam sites on the Internet (or Chapter 9 of this book) well knows. Jack Collom of Boulder, Colorado, two-time winner of a National Endowment for the Arts award, is only one of the more credentialed of Spam poets. The following six Spam acrostics were among twelve Collom once gave to John Lehndorff, food editor of the *Boulder Daily Camera* and a self-proclaimed Spam fan, who ran all twelve in the newspaper.

S econd World War's
P opular
A nimal-based
M ixture

S tyle
P roclaims
A
M oratorium.

S uddenly masked hombres seized
P etunia Pig
A nd
M ade her into a sort of dense Jell-O.

But the story doesn't end there. Shortly after a couple of Jack Collom's Spam acrostics appeared in the July 3, 1994, *New York Times Magazine* cover article, they popped up in a story in the *Star*, a supermarket tabloid. Headlined "Poet Gets $30,000 to Write Ditties about Spam!" and strategically placed next to a photo of Hulk Hogan, the story began:

> A poet is penning odes to the most famous luncheon meat in the world—and the federal government has paid $30,000 of your tax dollars for his Spam sonnets. Jack Collom, of Boulder, Colo., likes nothing better than sitting at home and rhapsodizing about the Hormel Company's top-selling product.
> And the National Endowment for the Arts finds his work so appetizing it has awarded Collom two fellowships, for $10,000 and $20,000.

The story reproduced a couple of the poems along with comments from Congressman Jack Kingson. "This is outrageous," Kingson is quoted

The Spam article in the July 3, 1994, *New York Times Magazine* started out as a one-paragraph piece on a superstition against carrying pork over a certain Hawaiian highway, but, with the encouragement of amused editors, it grew to fill four full pages and take over the cover. Author Judith Stone, whose work has appeared in many national magazines, says that no other article she has ever written has generated more positive phone calls and mail—including praise from *New York Times* publisher Arthur Ochs Sulzberger Jr. himself.

THE UNITED STATES OF SPAM
This prototypical American food saved the Soviet Army.
In 1994, more than 60 million Americans will eat it.
It makes good furniture polish. Also bait.
34 questions you never thought to ask.
BY JUDITH STONE

as saying. "If we weren't talking about the NEA, this would sound like a bunch of baloney."

Of course, the real baloney (or should we say luncheon meat?) was the *Star*'s attempt to turn Collom into another Robert Mapplethorpe or Karen Finley: Collom's NEA grants were awarded not for his Spam ditties, as the *Star* contended, but, in large part, for what he describes as some "fairly complex ecology pieces" he wrote years before he thought to do anything with Spam but eat it.

THE SPAM-IGNORANT LAMA Ogden Nash wrote verses about many subjects, but he particularly liked poking fun at the inanities of modern urban culture. Food was also a favorite subject, especially when it did not live up to his high standards. Spam took its hit in "I Will Arise and Go Now," a poem about a lama blissfully ignorant of consumer culture. Its title and tone make it a fitting conclusion to this chapter:

*In far Tibet
There live a lama,
He got no poppa,
Got no momma,*

*He got no wife,
He got no chillun,
Got no use
For penicillun,*

*He got no soap,
He got no opera,
He don't know Irium
From copra,*

*He got no songs,
He got no banter,
Don't know Jolson,
Don't know Cantor,*

*He got no teeth,
He got no gums,
Don't eat no Spam,
Don't need no Tums.*

*Indeed, the
Ignorant Have-Not
Don't even know
What he don't got.*

*If you will mind
The Philco, comma,
I think I'll go
And join that lama.*

Celebrating SPAM

eing a Spam fan in a society of nutrition nuts can get lonely. Fortunately there are occasions in this country when people can come out of the cupboard with their love of Spam luncheon meat and not be condemned to a lifetime of solo suppers, occasions when it's even okay to make fun of it because you're among people who understand. We're talking about the many events celebrating Spam that are now held across our great land.

Unlike festivals associated with other brand-name products, most Spam events are grassroots efforts, wafting naturally, like the smell of Spam when you open the can, out of people's love for the "Hormel meat of many uses." At these events, Spam is transformed from mere foodstuff into the rallying point for fun and cre-

ativity in fields as diverse as the fine arts and athletics.

Because most Spam festivals are unauthorized, one-time events and therefore, unlike Spam, ephemeral, we'll take a look at those three that by nature of their size and age will most likely still be going on by the time you read this book. They are the Spam Carving Contest in Seattle, the Spamarama in Austin, Texas, and the Spam Jam in Austin, Minnesota—hereafter to be collectively known as the Spam Festival Triumvirate.

SPAM, SPAM, SPAM, Espresso and SPAM

In a ranking of Seattle's most popular foodstuffs, Spam would have to take a backseat to expensive

The SPAM Festival Triumvirate

❏ Spam Carving Contest and Museum, Pioneer Square, Seattle, Washington; annually on a Saturday in February as part of the city's Fat Tuesday celebrations.

❏ Spamarama, Auditorium Shores, Austin, Texas; annually on a Saturday near April Fools' Day.

❏ Spam Jam, East Side Lake, Austin, Minnesota; annually on the Fourth of July weekend.

espresso and microbrewery beer. But it reigns supreme as a medium of artistic expression there. Proof is in the Spam Carving Contest held in the center city annually since 1990.

Contest founder Ruby Montana says the idea came to her one night in a dream, and if you've ever seen Montana's gift shop of pop-culture kitsch, it's easy to believe she would dream of Spam. For the first eight years of the contest, Montana's cosponsor was the city's equally offbeat Underground Tour, a tourist attraction that explores the city's history from the bottom up—literally. The T-shirt produced for the first Spam Carving Contest pretty much summed up the partnership with its cartoon of cowgirl Montana trying to lasso an uncooperative Spam can from the back of her rat steed.

Emcee Dana Cox signals the start of Seattle's 1993 Spam Carving Contest.

The carving contest borrows its beginning from the Miss America Pageant, with the ritual return of the previous year's winner adorned in a blue-and-yellow cape, wearing a crown fashioned from Spam cans, and waving a pig-bedecked scepter. Contestants, usually numbering about a hundred, are then given two cans of Spam and fifteen minutes to create a piece of sculpture with a plastic knife or whatever tool they bring with them. Garlic presses,

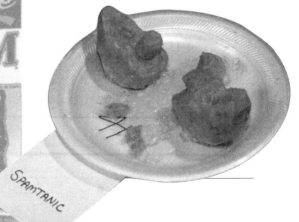

The author judging the 1994 Seattle Spam Carving Contest with novelist Tom Robbins.

cheese slicers, dental implements, and even hand drills have been used before; organizers draw the line at power saws. The competition takes place outside for obvious reasons. When the contestants open all their cans at once, Montana says, "It's a little like the running of the bulls."

Past winners of the judges' or People's Choice awards have included *Spamhenge, Spammy Wynette*

Singing *"Stand by Your Spam," Spamtom of the Opera, O.J. on the Spam,* and the Marcel Duchamp-esque *Spam Descending a Staircase.* Rare is the year when there isn't at least one entry depicting Uncle Spam, Abraspam Lincoln, the Spamtue of Liberty, or its Seattle equivalent, the Spam Needle.

Russ Leno, who won top prize in 1993 for a meaty depiction of a man entering Hades called *Going to Hell in a Spam Basket,* says the idea and title of a sculpture are

Carving Out Victory on the SPAM Sculpture Circuit: Tips from a Past Winner

"Spam's a pretty good medium for carving," says Russ Leno (no relation to Jay). He should know. Not only did Leno win the Seattle Spam Carving Contest once and show twice; he also carves ice and pumpkins, and he's coholder of the record for the world's longest sand sculpture (twenty-three miles).

"I started with wood, but it took too long," he explains. "Now I'm into biodegradable substances—things that melt, smell, and shrivel." With such substances, Leno advises, "your sculpture will look better if it's fresher." So if you're in a Spam carving contest that puts contestants through in batches, as in Seattle, try to compete in one of the later groupings.

Some other Spam sculpting tips from the champ:

❑ Be on the lookout for gristle. "It's like the grain in wood. You have to carve with it or you'll end up with pockmarks."

❑ Use a good sharp knife.

❑ Don't throw away the gelatin. It makes great glue for attaching parts, especially if it's left out to dry a bit.

❑ Think up the concept and name for your sculpture ahead of time, draw a sketch, then try carving it at least once before the big day. Leno always makes a little ritual of his dress rehearsal the night before the Seattle contest. He's not normally a Spam eater, but after he comes up with a sculpture he thinks could win, he takes some of the leftovers from his practice carving, mixes them with cheese and seasonings, spreads the mixture on toast, and becomes one with his medium—"for good luck," he says.

at least as important as the artistic execution. For instance, judges—who have included novelist Tom Robbins, *Northern Exposure* actor John Corbett, and rock star Duffy Bishop—gave an honorable mention to a smear of Spam on a plate called *Spamless in Seattle* in 1994 (with a nod to Tom Hanks's 1993 hit movie *Sleepless in Seattle*), and the People's Choice Award in 1995 went to a gel-to-block metamorphosis entitled the *Evolution of Spam.* Topical entries are also much admired. In 1993, one contestant formed a congressman out of the Spam brick and some soldiers out of the Spam gelatin and labeled it *Senator Spam Nunn Opposes Glaze in the Military.* After the announcement and

A sculpture of Spammy Wynette singing "Stand by Your Spam" made Angela Follett the 1992 Seattle carving queen.

crowning of the new winner (first prize is a nothing-to-joke-about pair of free airline tickets), the entries are placed on display in a storefront "museum" along with larger, even more serious tributes to Spam created by chefs and real gallery-showing artists. Past entries in this professional category have included a fantasy *Spaminaugural Dinner* (in honor of the junk-food-loving President Clinton); a Spam-covered, man-sized replica of the Seattle Art Museum's *Hammering Man* called *Spammering Man;* a pig-grease-stained mock-sacred *Shroud of Spam;* and a stained-glass depiction of football player Brian "Boz" Bosworth created by placing dyed headcheese, spaghetti, and Spam under Plexiglas.

The last sculpture was so impressive that it was stolen, and despite Ruby Montana's tearful pleas on local TV that *St. Boz, Martyr of the Turf Wars* would never survive without freeze-drying, it was never returned. A similar calamity befell Lorraine Howlett's 1995 prizewinning sculpture of her pit bull Sandy. The sculpture was supposed to remain on exhibit at the Spam Museum for two days, but when Howlett brought Sandy in to admire his salivating image, he wolfed it down.

The Other Austin's Meat Meet

In most places in Texas, Spam is served with eggs, in sandwiches, in macaroni casseroles and the like. Not so in Austin. At the Spamarama there Spam on the half shell, Spam caviar, Spam truffles, Spam escargot, Spamoni ice cream, Spam tequila, and moo goo gai Spam are more the order of the day.

The granddaddy of the big Spam festivals began in 1978 as a "slap in the jowls" at all the chili cook-offs in Texas. (Organizers didn't know at the time that Spam was made in the "sister city" of Austin, Minnesota.) "To me, chili's chili," says contest cofounder David Arnsberger. "Anybody can make a good one." But to make a great Spam dish,

Peggy Maceo called her Spamarama cook-off entry Baby Jane's Lunch.

chicken cordon bleu, beef Wellington, and crawfish étouffée. But the event quickly evolved into an anything-goes marathon of luncheon meat merriment and music attracting some eight thousand people and raising up to twenty thousand dollars for United Cerebral Palsy.

Nowadays you're more likely to encounter the hilarious than the haute at the "world-famous, Austintatious" Spamarama. One year, for instance, the cooking contest entrants in one booth were serving ice cream Spamwiches, with or without extra gelatin, to a surprising number of enthusiastic recipients, while next door to them

"now that really takes a chef."

In fact, early contestants were mainly professional chefs from the area's fanciest restaurants who substituted Spam for the usual meat in classical dishes like

a group of women dressed in Girl Scout uniforms handed out Spamores. Another year some Spamaramaniacs got into the spirit of the recovery movement by fitting out their booth with fake drug paraphernalia and funny-looking cigarettes stuffed with Spam under a sign that read: "Spam. The Big Lie. I lost my job, my wife, the love of my children. Spam ruined my life. Call the Spam Hot Line."

The official Spamarama cook-off contest rules capture the flavor of an event that has inspired such creations as Swineapple Upside-Down Cake, Piggy Pâté, and Spamuel Addams Austin Hogger Beer (described as a "somewhat pig-culiar amber malt"). One rule requires that, on request, contestants taste their dishes before the judges do. A second insists that they sign a statement absolving Spamarama sponsors of responsibility for "any injury, loss of property, loss of reputation, or any indigestion, gastronomic disturbances, or miasmic emissions which may be incurred during the event."

The entry form, com-

Piggy Pâté

This recipe comes from David Arnsberger and John Booher's comprehensive *Spamarama: The Cookbook.* Impress your friends by molding the pâté into the shape of a pig, as cook-off competitors Susan Sherwood and Jim Shaw did in 1996.

$1/2$ pound chicken livers
1 (12-ounce) can Spam or Spam Lite
    luncheon meat
2 tablespoons butter
2 cloves garlic, minced
1 onion, chopped
1 celery stalk, chopped
$1/4$ cup dry white wine
2 tablespoons brandy
1 teaspoon savory
Thyme
Paprika
Salt
Pepper
4 tablespoons sour cream

Clean and remove fat from chicken livers; set aside. Cut Spam into chunks. Melt butter in large skillet and sauté garlic, onion, and celery until soft. Add livers and cook 5 to 10 minutes. Add Spam and cook another 5 to 10 minutes, blending well. Add wine, brandy, and savory. Season with thyme, paprika, salt, and pepper to taste. Blend in food processor until smooth. Add sour cream and process again briefly. Transfer to bowl, cover, and chill overnight. Serve with crackers.

posed in the same spirit, requests the name of a person to contact in case of indigestion and provides the names of judges to be bribed. Those who have been on the receiving end of Spamarama payola include syndicated newspaper columnist Molly Ivins, ex–Lyndon Johnson aide Liz Carpenter, and a local city councilman. (Another enterprising local politician once campaigned at the event by handing out pieces of Spam cut in the shape of bells, symbolizing his commitment to fight rate increases by Southwestern Bell.)

John Myers, former executive chef at Austin's fancy Driskill Hotel and a seven-time winner of the coveted Spamerica's Cup, top prize in the Spamarama cook-off, says that one of the key ingredients to success is presentation—and by "presentation" he means dressing up like Jim and Spammy Bakker to warn against the evils of deviled Spam, not dressing a plate with a few sprigs of parsley. Myers learned this lesson the hard way in 1988 when employees of the Texas Chili Parlor, dressed in fatigues and camouflage, waving toy machine guns, and lobbing cans of Spam like frag-

The strange creature behind Wayne Roberts' Spam-a-gator Gumbo, a 1995 Spamarama award winner.

Chef John Myers with the Spam sculpture he created by taking a chainsaw to a three-hundred-pound block of blue ice.

Lights, Camera, SPAM

All three of the big Spam festivals have had their fifteen seconds of fame on the network news shows. But only the Spamarama in Austin, Texas, has the distinction of inspiring a movie.

Director-writer Cressandra Thibodeaux says she first became aware of Spam as a cultural icon when she read a graffito in the bathroom of the Magnolia Café in Austin: "I'm pink, therefore I'm Spam." She soon learned of Austin's Spamarama festival and enlisted *Slacker* and *Dazed and Confused* photo director Lee Daniels to shoot some footage of it for her in 1995.

Thibodeaux initially intended the footage to be part of a documentary about wacky festivals. But meeting charismatic Spamarama festival director David Arnsberger

inspired her to pursue a full-length feature. "Maybe I was drunk, but I kept thinking, 'He should be in a movie,'" Thibodeaux told the *Austin American-Statesman.* So she wrote a fictionalized script around the documentary footage already shot and got Arnsberger, a group of his Spamarama colleagues, and some out-of-work actors to play the parts.

Spamarama: The Movie stars Joe Stevens as a champion Spam chili maker named Bird who works for a pizza delivery chain that requires employees to dress up like the chain's mascot, a lizard. The movie served as Thibodeaux's thesis for a graduate degree in film from Columbia, and it's hard to say whether it will ever be seen by anyone besides her professors. But if Thibodeaux learned anything at all about Spam during the filming, she'll never be a starving artist.

mentation grenades, stole the Spamerica's Cup from him with their Spamdinista Chili. A much wiser man because of the defeat, Myers regained the top prize the following year as the Spamatollah.

Cooking is not the only fun to be had at the Spamarama. Since 1990 the festival has also been the proud spon-

sor of the Spamalympics. Otherwise known as the Pigathlon, the Spamalympics consists of four events. The Spam Cram tests how fast competitors can eat a Spamburger containing an entire twelve-ounce block of meat. The second event, the Spam Call, resembles a hog call, only the call is directed at a can of Spam and is judged by audience acclamation. Contestants usually win by telling stories or singing songs—"Spammy" by Spam Jolson, for instance, or "Pigaro" by Spamiano Spamarotti.

The third event is the Spam Toss, which is similar to an egg toss except that the object tossed is a

---

The Spam Toss: A contestant prepares to receive.

hunk of America's favorite luncheon meat coated with gelatin. Finally, there's the Spam Relay, a timed race in which each member of a team of four must carry a Spam block baton forty yards and then take a bite out of it before handing it off to a teammate. One relay participant actually passed out during the 1997 competition (whether from the heat, the physical exertion, or some other aspect of the event, no one is sure). And this was not the first Spamalympics medical incident. Mark Carey suffered a pulled leg muscle while winning the 1991 contest because he didn't have time to stretch out before the event. "I was inside ordering a beer," he explained to the reporter who chronicled his victory.

Indeed, Spamarama was for years held in or around Austin bars, and alcohol is an integral part of its freewheeling character. You'd almost have to be drunk to dream up some of the most memorable

cooking contest entries. They include Spamalamadingdongs (bite-sized Spam sandwiches covered with whipped cream and chocolate), Spam Quiche Lorena Bobbitt (use your imagination), and Spampers (ditto!).

Hometown Proud

Held every Fourth of July weekend in conjunction with Austin's Spam Town USA Festival, the Spam Jam is the one and only Spam festival endorsed and run by the Spam makers at Hormel Foods. As such, it's definitely a family affair, and the activities it sponsors are only in the best of taste. In fact, to those fun makers who attend the Spam event in the other Austin, this one might seem a bit strait-

laced. Whereas the Spam Toss in Texas, for instance, involves hurling perfectly good food through the air and (ultimately) onto the ground, here it entails respectfully pitching rings over Spam cans.

Other Spam Jam activities show a similar reverence for the hometown meat that made good. For example, no one competing in the Spam Fishing Contest would ever think of using Spam as bait—despite the name of the event and the luncheon meat's famed effectiveness as a lure. Nor should you bother asking if the gelatin used in the Spam Gelatin Jump, one of the Spam Family Fun Games, comes from Spam cans. It doesn't, and in these parts the question is considered strange.

Although the first official Spam Jam was held in 1991, the festival has its roots in Austin's homage to the luncheon meat's fiftieth birthday in 1987. City leaders were hoping the celebration would help mend a community that had been deeply divided by the 1985–86 meatpackers strike against Hormel. But the seams showed when some ex-strikers allegedly stole a gold Spam medallion that was to have been the focus of a treasure hunt, and others arranged an alternative event just outside town honoring Local P-9 and organized labor in general.

Hormel waited four years before attempting another public festival, this time on the occasion of the company's hundredth anniversary. The 1991 Spam Jam was similar to the current one except that it had a longer name (the Spam Jamboree), it was part of a celebration known as Cedar River Days

These lean, muscular physiques may explain why the Spam Jam 5-Mile Run is no longer called the Hog Jog.

(now called the Spam Town USA Festival), and it included Spam sculpting and Spam eating contests. The Spam sculpting contest was eliminated after that first year, possibly because *Harper's* published the sculpting rules underneath the smart-alecky headline "But Is It Food?" The Spam eating contest was eliminated a year later, after a 220-pound truck driver with no teeth captured the top prize by eating two Spamburger hamburgers and drinking one eight-ounce glass of water in sixty-four seconds. Hormel spokesman V. Allan Krejci said the contest, in retrospect, did not seem to be "in good taste."

So what does Hormel Foods consider tasty—er, tasteful? Certainly local celebrities such as Miss Austin, Jay Hormel's son James (who showed up in 1998), and Mr. and Mrs. Spam (a couple who walk around in giant Spam can costumes) pass the test. So do the annual foodfests, such as the Spam

The Man inside the Can

It started with Mickey Mouse. Now there are hundreds of costumed characters creating goodwill—and new business—for corporations at fairs, festivals, and parades across the country. Mr. Spam is one of them.

For more than six years the man in the Mr. Spam costume was cellular phone salesman Gary Ludwig. The first-ever and therefore the most experienced Mr. Spam, Gary shed his container one day to talk about life inside the can.

Q. How did you get the job?

A. It was during the planning meetings for the Cedar River Days celebration [now the Spam Town USA Festival, which includes the Spam Jam]. They had come up with this costume for a caricature of Spam. Someone said, "Yeah, but who can we get to put on a red leotard?" I understand two or three people answered at once, "Gary will do it."

Q. What's it like in there?

A. There's a harness built into the can that rests on your shoulders, and there's a belt that goes around your waist that supports the weight—it weighs about fifteen pounds. There's a built-in fan and a shelf for a bottle of water or Gatorade, which I sip with a straw. I blink the eyes by pulling on a rope.

Q. What are the most annoying things people do to you?

A. Some people will come up and put their face right up to one of the eyes and make faces. They'll feel up my arm to see if somebody's really in there. Once there was a food demonstration here in town and there was a crowd of little old ladies pressing in and around me and all of a sudden I felt a pinch on my butt. . . . When you put on the feet and the can, you're really not a person anymore.

Q. Who's the most famous person you ever met as Mr. Spam?

A. Once I got on an elevator at a convention in Saint Paul dressed in my leotard with the can at my side, and a gentleman started asking me about the product. He said he was a writer. We conversed to the bottom of the elevator. Later I found an autographed copy of *All I Really Need to Know I Learned in Kindergarten* tucked into one of the costume straps.

Breakfast and the Pork Producers Supper, and the activities that have been part of the celebration since the beginning: the 5-Mile Run (formerly the Hog Jog), the Friend-ship Bike Ride to Browns-dale (formerly to Moscow, a nearby town of one), the Milk Carton Boat Race, and the Spam Recipe Contest.

Music also seems to meet the company's standards. For several years a group called the Teddy Bears played at the Spam Jam, and

A Tale of Two SPAM-Loving Country Singers

When Trace Adkins was driving through southern Minnesota one day in the fall of 1996 as part of the promotional tour for his country music album *Dreamin' Out Loud,* he asked his driver to stop at Hormel Foods Corporation in Austin. Adkins had eaten a lot of Spam growing up in rural Sarepta, Louisiana, and he was curious to see how it was made. However, because he had not called ahead and was not lucky enough to get a Hormel Foods security guard who knew anything about country music, he was sent away.

Not until the company's public relations department received phone calls inquiring about the snub did the folks there realize that they had unwittingly insulted an unpaid endorser of Spam and one of country music's brightest rising stars. When they did, they quickly made it up to Adkins by sending him a boxload of Spam merchandise and an invitation to perform at the 1997 Spam Jam.

T. Graham Brown is another country singer with a passion for Spam. Best known for such '80s hits as "I Wish I Could Hurt That Way Again," Brown calls his back-up band Rack of Spam, and he regularly wore a solid gold Spam key around his neck until it fell down the bathtub drain in a motel in Raleigh, North Carolina. Brown fans still sometimes stack cans of Spam

Spam-appreciatin' T. Graham Brown.

on the corners of stages where he performs—like offerings on an altar. Although he has never been paid to sing or talk about Spam the way he's been paid to sing about Taco Bell (in its "Run for the Border" ads), Brown ate a lot of the luncheon meat growing up and seems to understand it perfectly. As he says, Spam is "an everyman kind of food."

the 1997 festival featured the Killer Hay Seeds, the Whitesidewalls, and Trouble Shooter along with country-and-western star Trace Adkins, a self-proclaimed "Spam junkie." But year in and year out, the performers who most satiate this crowd's hunger for music are the Spamettes, a group of four local women who sing solely of Spam.

The Spamettes' repertoire includes show tunes like "Spamalot" (sung to the tune of "Camelot"), movie theme songs like "Spam Is a Many-Splendored Thing," and such old favorites as "Mr. Spamman"
("Mr. Sandman") and "Don't Go Eatin' a Can of Spam" ("Don't Sit under the Apple Tree").

Although the quartet is normally accompanied only by Krista Bergman on keyboard, Amy Baskin on drums, and Theresa Iverson on bass, three of them—Sonia Larson, Holly Dalager, and Nancy Heimer—bring out tom-toms and sticks when the fourth, Denise Condon, belts out "Spa-a-am O," launching into the calypso. The Spamettes also ham it up while singing parodies of other popular tunes, donning yellow kitchen gloves for "Stop in the Name of Spam" and John Lennon–style glasses for "Hey Dude."

The group was created to perform at the 1991 Spam Jamboree. Nancy Burger, a local school music teacher, had been put in charge of entertainment for the festival and was looking for some kind of comic act when she heard that Larson, the wife of a Hormel purchasing agent, had written a Spam parody of Tammy Wynette's "Stand by Your Man." "She was embarrassed about it. But I said it was exactly what we needed," recalls Burger. Since everybody knows everybody else in a small town like Austin, and everybody has some connection to Hormel, it didn't take long for Burger and Larson to find Condon and Dori Schou. And the original Spamettes were born.

What started as a pickup group to perform at that one Spam Jam has turned into a steady moonlighting job for old-timers Larson and Condon and newcomers Dalager and Heimer, who have replaced Burger and Schou. The Spamettes perform throughout the

The Spamettes (from left to right): Holly Dalager, Sonia Larson, Denise Condon, and Nancy Heimer.

The original Spamettes (from left to right): Sonia Larson, Nancy Burger, Denise Condon, and Dori Schou.

"SPAM on the Range"

These lyrics for the Spamettes' takeoff on the cowboy favorite "Home on the Range" were written by Denise Condon.

Oh give me some Spam
With that grand monogram
So my pantry will have a supply
Of that Spam luncheon meat
(Made in our county seat)
That they oft try to vilify.

Spam, Spam on the range,
Though the looks they may give you
are strange,
Don't ever deny
That the taste makes you high,
And you see no good reason to
change.

year for area civic and women's clubs, and they've even worked up a program of Spam Christmas favorites that includes "Cans of Spam" (sung to the tune of "Jingle Bells"), "Spam Hot Dish" ("White Christmas"), "Up on the Stovetop" ("Up on the Housetop"), and "What Meat Is This," a seculiarized version of "What Child Is This" with the following refrain:

> *Spam, Spam, it's the food of kings.*
> *It's the luncheon meat that the*
> *whole world brings*
> *To ev-e-ry smorgasbord.*
> *It's the food that is the most*
> *adored.*

Larson and Condon write most of the lyrics. As Larson explained to a reporter for the *Los Angeles Times,* "I have a boring life." Maybe so, but the Spamettes do anything but bore the crowds at the Spam Jam. They're now so popular that they have to give more than one performance and are even being asked to autograph Spam boxer shorts (brand-new ones, of course, fresh out of the package). In fact, the Spamettes are probably no small part of the reason that more than twenty thousand people attend the Spam Jam annually and that the event has twice been named one of the top twenty-five tour group attractions in all of Minnesota.

Opera singer Marilyn Brustadt directs the national Spamthem at the 1983 Colorado Spamposium, attended by (among others) the driver of a camper rigged out like a can of Spam with Cheese Chunks.

Other SPAM Events: An Incomplete History

Since there has never been an official registry of Spam events, nobody knows exactly when the first one was held or how many have taken place since then. In the unofficial annals of Spamfoolery, however, the following stand out:

❑ July 23, 1983: Advertising man Lewis Cady of Denver, Colorado, hosted the First Ever Spamposium, a gathering of thirty-three-odd (and we do mean odd) Spam scholars who delivered papers from a beer-filled refrigerator-podium. Highlights included the singing of "The Star-Spamgled Banner," a demonstration of Do Spam Key (a martial art that involves smashing Spam slices against one's forehead), a noisy experiment testing the

Hearts of SPAM

Spamposium czar Lewis Cady serves these Spam hearts at a champagne reception for stars of the Central City opera festival in Colorado every summer. But they would also make an attractive Valentine's Day appetizer.

    1 (12-ounce) can Spam luncheon meat
    Oil for frying

    Cut Spam into rectangular slices about 5/16 inch thick. Cut each slice in half diagonally and then slice little triangles out of the rounded corner of each half. Drop heart-shaped Spamettes into hot frying pan. Cover and fry until crisp like bacon. Serve piping hot.

The giant hanging Spam can and poster that heralded the 1985 Spam exhibit at the Rhode Island College Art Center.

hypothesis that the nitrite in Spam points to its original use as an explosive, a recitation of the epic poem *Grease Wars,* and a historical treatise on Custer's Last Spam (at which Native Americans made processed pork of the pesky army general).

❑ February 1985: Art student Sean Harrington organized the First (and last) Annual Spam Exhibition at the Rhode Island College Art Center in Providence. Beating out some thirty other entrants, Paul Chabot won first prize, a twenty-dollar gift certificate from an art store, for a pair of pen-and-ink drawings in which certain parts of the anatomy had been replaced by Spam. Second prize was a Spam casserole. Third prize was two Spam casseroles. After the exhibit, Harrington proposed to a fellow organizer with a Spam can pull-tab engagement ring, and she accepted.

❑ May 1987: The Golden Gate Bridge and Spam both turned fifty at the same time, and Sausalito, California, decided to celebrate the coincidence by enlisting architect Michael Rex to build a twenty-foot-tall sculpture of the Golden Gate's north tower entirely out of Spam cans. Created by gluing thirty-five hundred Hormel-donated empty cans to a plywood frame with "buckets and buckets of rubber cement," *Spam Span* served as a dazzling backdrop to three days of food (including Spam sandwiches) and fun (including a costume party where a couple came as Spam

and Wonder bread) before being destroyed for lack of storage space.

❏ June 1988: The theater department at Seattle Pacific University began an annual tradition of handing out Seattle Pacific Artistic Merit, or Golden Spam, Awards for such dubious theatrical achievements as portraying the most characters who die (the Meet the Reaper Award) or wearing the most interesting wigs (the Hair Today Gone Tomorrow Award). Most recipients get a pedestal-mounted can of regular Spam, but the award for most distinguished walk-on features a can of Spam Lite, and the consolation prize for any graduating senior who has failed to win a single Golden Spam is a tiny tin of Spam Spread.

❏ May 1989: Inspired by Hawaii Governor John Waihee's declaration that

bedded to a charity sporting event at Punai Hu High School, where it was devoured by a ravenous crowd.

❏ April 1990: Carnegie-Mellon University senior Derek Chung hosted Spamfest VI, his sixth love feast of Spam, Twinkies, and soda. Billing it as the "premier pork event of the university," Chung lured fifty fellow students to his apartment with free helpings of Spam pizza, Spamwiches, macaroni and Spam, and Spam and eggs. Chung explained the attraction this way: "Spam partially fills you up and partially you just don't want to eat much of it."

❏ October 1992: Spam was awarded an Ig Nobel Prize for Nutrition by the editors of the *Journal of Irreproducible Results* (now called the *Annals of Improbable Research*, or *AIR*). Nobel laureates attending the awards ceremony at Massachusetts Institute of Technology marked the moment by eating Spam sandwiches on stage.

❏ February 1994: In honor of a colleague who admitted to once believing that Spam came from Spam animals, hairdressers at the Visions of You Hair Studio in Collinsville, Illinois, donned "Save the Spam" T-shirts—depicting a creature with horns, a bill, a curly pig tail, webbed feet, and spots—and served Spam meatballs, Spam fondue, and other Spam delights free with every haircut.

SPAMAGEDDON

Spam musubi (a type of sushi made with Spam) was his favorite food, a Honolulu radio station sponsored the first Spam Pro Am, a Spam musubi–making contest. Patrick Nowack of the French Gourmet catering company rose to the occasion by creating the world's largest Spam musubi, and the one-ton monster was flat-

❏ April 1994: Some Monty Python fans at the University of California in Santa Cruz attempted to add an artistic dimension to an all-cement residential college by creating a Spam can tree and launching Spam on Cement, an annual music festival that once featured Punk Rock Patty, an eighty-year-old vocalist with pink hair and fishnet stockings. Across the country that same month, members of a Swarthmore College science fiction and fantasy club who apparently could not quite believe that Spam exists dipped some in liquid nitrogen and dropped it from the third floor of a college building, thereby inaugurating a series of annual "Spamageddon" events that have involved building a Spamapult out of rope, a crutch, and some two-by-fours; organizing a Spam shot put competition; devising a Spam and potato cannon; and creating a Spamyata—a pig-shaped piñata filled with diced Spam.

❑ April 1, 1995: Rachelle's on the River, a fine dining establishment in Saint Clair, Michigan, chose April Fools' Day to shine the culinary spotlight on Spam. Showcasing Spam under glass at the entrance and providing a podium for spontaneous Spamdimonials in the dining room, the restaurant served some seventy-five of its five Spam dinner specials—including a Star-Spamgled Banner appetizer—and got one application for employment.

❑ September 15–19, 1995: The Liberty House chain of fancy Hawaiian department stores hosted the Spamboree Jamboree. During the week-long celebration, store employees wearing Spam musubi costumes danced to Spam songs, Jim "Gomer Pyle" Nabors and other local celebrities created Spam table settings, and top Pacific Rim chefs cooked up such gourmet Spam dishes as spicy fish and Spam cassoulet, Cajun Spam Benedict, Spam bruschetta, and Spam pot-stickers.

❑ June 22, 1996: Bob Crane, who describes himself as "the manliest florist in the Pacific Northwest," masterminded the first annual Manly Men Parade and Spam Festival in Roslyn, Washington (the little town

that served as the setting for *Northern Exposure*). After a camping trip in the Cascade Mountains, thirty-nine members of the Order of the Manly Men emerged from the woods to parade down Main Street with their biker babes and first-born sons, the pink-prom-dress-clad Spam Queen and her court, a Spammobile (constructed by placing a six-foot plywood Spam can on a riding lawn mower), and some half a dozen people dressed in Spam can costumes. In honor of the occasion, all six local restaurants added Spam specials to their menus, there was a Spam cook-off, and Spam marshals imposed a twenty-five-cent fine on anyone caught making derogatory remarks about the Manly Men's meat of choice.

❑ August 22, 1997: Reasoning that Spam *is* ground hog, banker Bob Brandt of Unadilla, Nebraska, renamed his ten-year-old Groundhog Classic Golf Tournament the Spam Groundhog Classic and started luring entrants with a free can of Spam instead of a free sleeve of golf balls. Refreshments that year featured Spam sandwiches with onions, jalapeños, and horseradish, resulting in what Brandt says was "the highest consumption of beer in all my years of doing this tournament."

The Craven sisters contributing some Spam spirit to the first Manly Men Parade in Roslyn, Washington.

CyberSPAM

In 1998, a quest for Spam sites on the Internet using the Yahoo! search service yielded almost 400 references. About 70 percent of those led to sites about spamming, an Internet term for electronic junk mail. But the remaining 30 percent—some 120 sites—still represent about twice as much Internet interest as there is in Marilyn Monroe and about four times as much as there is in Bruce Springsteen. What's more, Net surfers go to the Spam sites in droves. Take Find-the-Spam, for example. Before this Internet game had even celebrated its second anniversary on the World Wide Web, it had gotten nearly a million "hits."

According to the author of an on-line guide called the Useless Pages, food is the most popular topic of pointless sites on the Internet, and Spam luncheon meat is the most popular food "by far." Why is a luncheon meat that's been around for more than sixty years so big with cyberspace travelers? Professor Dinty Moore, author of *The Emperor's Virtual Clothes: The Naked Truth about Internet Culture,* says it's because of that zany bunch of Brits known as Monty Python: The troupe's intellectual brand of humor appeals to the left-brain computer nerds who frequent the Internet.

The Net's Dirty Word

Certainly the electronic community's use of *spam* to refer to the indiscriminate posting or cross-posting of advertising throughout cyberspace supports Moore's hypothesis: It has its source in the famous Monty Python sketch about the café with the nearly all-Spam menu. "The repetition of the word *Spam* in the sketch mimics the repetition of electronic messages," says Moore (who, in case you were wondering, was named after a character in the comic strip *Bringing Up Father* rather than for that other popular Hormel Foods product of the masses, Dinty Moore stew).

Although none too happy about it, the makers of Spam have swallowed the cyberspace use of the word *spam* more easily than they have the use of the antispamming symbol of a circle with a slash over an image of a Spam can or the popular acronymic response to spam, ESAD—for "Eat Spam and die." Nor do they like sharing their trademarked name with the cybervillains who litter the information superhighway with junk e-mail. Nevertheless, the

Surfing the CyberSPAM Wave

You'll find the official Spam site maintained by Hormel Foods at www.spam.com. If you're interested in exploring the other Spam sites mentioned in this chapter, look for them at the following addresses. Remember, though, that the Internet, unlike Spam, is constantly changing. So by the time you read this, some of the sites may have disappeared or been moved to different shelves in the virtual cupboard.

Amazing Spam Home Page: http://www.cusd.claremont.edu/~mrosenbl/spam.html
Antics and Mayhem Page: http://www.be.com/~dbg/antics
Austin, Texas, Spamarama: http://www.spamarama.com
Church of Spam: http://www.grapevinenet.com/swiggy/spam
Culinary Connection: http://www.culinary.com
Dan Garcia's Spam Page: http://http.cs.berkeley.edu/~ddgarcia/spam.html
Exploding Spam Site: http://web.mit.edu/belg4mit/www/explod.html
Find-the-Spam: http://www.smalltime.com/nowhere/findthespam
Great Spam Debate: http://members.tripod.com/~zol/spam.html
John's Shrine to Spam: http://www.iconnect.net/home/jstrong/spam.html
Monty Python Spam Club: http://www.pythonline.com
Seattle Spam Carving Contest: http://www.rubymontana.com
Spam Bowling: http://www.octane.com/spambowl.html
Spam Cam: http://www.fright.com/spam/spamcam.html
Spam Center: http://members.xoom.com/brassman/spam
Spam Haiku Archive:: http://pemtropics.mit.edu/~jcho/spam
Spamily's Spam Page: http://www.vex.net/~emily/spam.html
Yeeeoww!!!: http://www.yeeeoww.com/spamentries.html

Every Spam is sacred.

www.clari.net
ClariNet

two Phoenix immigration lawyers first accused of spamming are commonly known as Crosspost and Spam, and the owner of America's most infamous bulk e-mail advertising firm (Sanford Wallace of Cyber Promotions) is called the Spam King.

Like John the Baptist, "Spam King" Sanford Wallace appears with his head on a platter at John's Shrine to Spam.

The Lovely SPAM, Wonderful SPAM Club

The Monty Python troupe itself has acknowledged the Spam skit–Internet connection by dubbing one section of its official Web site the Spam Club. Click on the icon of the people riding the pig and you'll come to a sign-up form asking for your name, e-mail address, and shoe size. If you feel so inclined, you can also let the club know whether you are over eighteen, oversexed, over the moon, or over hepatitis.

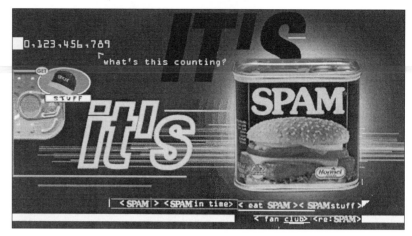

Once in the Spam Club, which was "founded in 1492 (and again in 1664)" and is "recommended by God," you can "escape the tyranny of boring old horoscopes" by changing your star sign to Spam, "the fastest growing pressed-meat star sign on the Internet." In addition, you can e-mail your eyebrows, kneecaps, toenails, and other body parts to needy recipients by availing yourself of the club's "ecologically sound and viable" organ recycling service.

And Now for Something Completely Tasteful

The Spam Club at the Monty Python site is not to be confused with the Official Spam Fan Club sponsored by Hormel Foods Corporation. For information about how to join this club, go to the company's Official Spam Home Page, where you can download the latest issue of the club's newsletter, *A Slice of Spam,* and amuse yourself in other ways as well. The site includes a multiple-choice Spam trivia quiz, an archive of Spam recipes that you can access by specifying the occasion and cooking method of your choice, and a section of FAQs (frequently asked questions), where you can find out, among other things, what little effect all the Spam jokes have had on company morale.

In the philosophical words of Spammy, the fan club's advice columnist, "Spam doesn't live in glass houses. It comes in cans."

And that's not all. "Spam in Time," the best part of the site, lets you take a virtual tour through the landscape of American pop culture from the perspective of someone obsessed with Spam. Remember that most famous line from that most famous movie of

1939? Well, through the lens of America's favorite luncheon meat, it's "Frankly, my dear, I'd love some Spam." And remember the slang term *groovy*? To a Spamaniac it was coined by a San Francisco teenager in the '60s to describe a Spam and cheese sandwich. In "Spam in Time" you can also watch a Spam can salute Chubby Checker by doing the twist, you can interactively dress a Spam can in an Afro, platform shoes, and other '70s gear, and, as a bonus, you can download some Spam desktop imagery to enjoy while you're away from the site.

An Internet SPAMpler

Besides the Official Spam Home Page, there are lots of interesting, if less sophisticated, unofficial Spam sites that have been developed by fans. Most of the general ones—among them Dan Garcia's Spam Page, the Amazing Spam Home Page, the Spam Center, and Spamily's Spam Page—serve as archives for Spam material collected from the now mostly inactive or spam-oriented alt.spam Internet discussion groups and other sources. At more than one of the sites, for example, you may encounter an academic paper arguing that the entire observable universe is actually a can of Spam or a *Dragnet* parody in which Friday and Gannon force an offending computer spammer to eat Spam. You may also encounter the full text (with or without sound bites) of the Monty Python Spam skit, excerpts from Weird Al Yankovic's "Spam" song, and an all-type rendering of a Spam can from the Internet's pregraphic age.

Spam fans who are a bit further along on the Spam information curve will find these general Web sites most useful for the links or pointers they provide to other, more specialized sites. A couple of the specialized sites allow you to take virtual trips to the Seattle and Austin, Texas, Spam festivals. Two others offer Spam recipes from opposite ends of the reality scale. At one end, the Culinary Connection's Spam Files include recipes for such delicacies as Spam jambalaya, Spam Wellington, and Spam strudel. The other end of the scale is represented by the aptly named Yecch!!! section of Yeeeoww!!! Digital Graphics Laboratories' site, which includes a recipe that calls for kryptonite and Superman as well as Spam. Still other specialized sites are devoted to Spam science and other Spam topics.

SPAM in the Cyberlab

The Antics and Mayhem Page produced by some ex–Silicon Graphics workers isn't exclusively about Spam, but its offerings include a pictorial record of an attempt to burn a block of Spam in the can with a Fresnel lens capable of reaching three thousand

SPAM as Bait for On-Line Customers

Fishermen have been using Spam to lure fish for years. In the fall of 1995 the folks at Prodigy decided to try using it to lure new subscribers to their on-line service. They created an ad illustrating how you could spend ten free hours on Prodigy exploring "your life-long fascination with Spam." The idea, according to Prodigy ad agency Cliff Freeman & Partners, was to get you thinking, "If there's *this* much about something as weird and specialized as Spam available through Prodigy, imagine how much

> *HOUR 1* **>** You've got 10 free hours on Prodigy. So naturally, you begin by exploring your lifelong fascination with SPAM® (a.k.a. "potted meat," "pink gold").

I'll find about the more normal thing I'm interested in."

What the ad doesn't tell you, of course, is that there's a lot more about Spam on the Internet than there is about other, more serious sub-jects. Nevertheless, you won't be able to have any long talks with "the notorious Spam sis-ters" on the Internet, as the ad suggests. Nor will you be able to discover the "dan-gerous number of people who named their children 'Spam.'" Freeman's David Angelo confesses to using "creative license" on those parts.

degrees Fahrenheit. In the accompanying text, Dominic Giampaolo writes, "As you can see, the result wasn't pretty (or appetizing). The Spam actu-ally caught fire several times." He goes on to boast that, despite having sat burnt and half opened in his office for months, the Spam block has yet to show "one sign of mold or decay."

At another site, the Spam Cam, kitchen scientist Dawn Groves conducted a whole series of Spam experiments over a period of more than two and a half years. Using a high-resolution video camera as her lab equipment, Groves attempted to answer the burning question How does Spam decompose com-pared to well-known junk foods? She has since grad-uated to creating "serious weird" games and stories for her Fright Site, so you can no longer check in for a daily update on the progress of her Spam Cam experiments. However, an archive containing all five of them is still available for cyberviewing. (A mile-stone event in the Spam Cam's history occurred when Groves inadvertently cut out of one day's pho-

tograph a marshmallow Easter chick that had long been part of an experiment. She reported receiving a staggering amount of e-mail the following day asking, "Where's the Peep?" "What happened to the Peep?" "The Peep is gone! Did it run away? Is it dead?")

If you're looking for a somewhat more flattering view of America's favorite luncheon meat in meta-morphosis, go to the Exploding Spam site, which offers a kinetic abstract art piece resembling Cracker Jack "wiggle" picture cards. At this site, you can see Spam cans dissolve and reassemble before your eyes.

SPAMoetry

Art of the poetical kind is the focus of the Spam Haiku Archive, a Web site created at the Arecibo Observatory in Puerto Rico in June 1995 "so that anyone who comes under the influence of this enigmatic porcine muse can share his/her poetic epiphany with the rest of the world." Although Spam haiku—Spamku, for short—has been e-mailed

The Dead-Meat Poets Society

John N. Cho estimates that about 95 percent of the thousands of Spam haiku in his archive are somewhat negative about the luncheon meat. He estimates that a similar percentage of his regular contributors (himself included) do not eat Spam. Could there be a connection? Maybe. Does it matter? Cho and his contributors seem to think not. These haiku "are not so much about eating Spam as the essence of Spam," offers Spam haikuist Kenneth S. Zuroski. "It's not even Spam per se. It seems to be a place holder on the page. It's an opportunity for critical thinking. It's a form of meditation."

The following choice cuts from Cho's archive illustrate the depth and breadth of Spam haiku thinking.

Man wearing white shirt
drops meat, causing greasy stain;
cries, "Out, out, Spam dot!"
　　—Francis Heaney

Murder mystery
solved: Colonel Mustard in the
ballroom with the Spam
　　—Chris Fishel

Burroughs plays William
Tell with Spam loaf, kills wife, in
Naked Luncheon Meat.
　　—John N. Cho

Gershwin devours Spam,
looks at can, writes "Rhapsody
in Blue and Yellow."
　　—Chris Fishel

"A Spam murder, Holmes?
Whither the murder weapon?"
"Alimentary."
　　—Ken Zuroski

Remember Meathead?
Chauvinist pig Archie?
All in the Spamily
　　—Neil Stallings and Martin Booda

Spock scans the pink meat.
"It's life, Jim," he tells Kirk, "but . . .
not as we know it."
　　—John M. Debevec

I'd love to see the
aurora boarealis—
the northern Spam Lites.
　　—Geoff Holme

Geometric meat
stacked so neatly on the shelf
pig squared—nth power
　　—Sarah Miller Arnold

Amspay aikuhay
ogicallay anguagelay:
igpay Atinlay
　　—Artinmay Oodabay

around the Internet for years and is featured on many general Spam pages, the site developed by atmospheric scientist

Spam Haiku Archive master John N. Cho.

John Nagamichi Cho—otherwise known as SHAM, for Spam Haiku Archive master—is the mother lode. After just three years on the Web,

Cho's archive had attracted some ten thousand Spamku and was being visited by about 150 people a day.

Why haiku? Cho says that the "postmodern, cross-cultural literary form" is perfect for our short-attention-span culture and that "adding the Spam element has the effect of collapsing serious and pop art." The campy potted pork subject matter makes people feel less intimidated about writing poetry, he contends, and the strict three-line structure of the haiku—five syllables, seven syllables, five syllables—appeals to rule-loving computer nerds.

But does Spamku really meet all the haiku rules? This urgent question was debated at length in a February 1996 article of the on-line *New York Times*. According to purists, the article soberly points out, "if a haiku is humorous, satiric or not about nature, it rightly should be called a senryu." By these rigid tone standards, there's no question that most Spamku should be reclassified as Spamryu. The subject matter criterion is another matter, though. Whether they're called Spamku or Spamryu, the poems are definitely about nature, says a Hormel Foods spokesperson: Spam "comes from a pig, which is as natural as it gets."

Honolulu Star-Bulletin columnist Charles Memminger also objects to Spam haiku, although not for any of the technical reasons cited in the *Times* article. Haiku is too "wimpy" for a product as important as Spam, says Memminger. It needs something grander to do it justice—an epic poem, for instance. Cho doesn't have anything quite that grand in his archive yet, but his collec-

Pig Newtons

This recipe from Page O' Spam, the Web site of a group of home brewers called the Boston Wort Processors, was created by Mary Anne McQuillan and Fred Sterner for the group's First Annual Spam and Beer Tasting.

1 (12-ounce) can Spam luncheon meat
1 can refrigerated crescent roll dough

Preheat oven to 350 degrees. Cut Spam in half, then in 1/4-inch slices. Unroll dough, separate into two long rectangles, and pat remaining perforations closed. Center Spam slices end to end down the length of each rectangle (reserving any leftover slices for another use). Fold sides of dough up over Spam and seal with fingers. Slice filled dough into sections the size of Fig Newtons and place seamside down on a cookie sheet. Bake 15 to 20 minutes or until golden brown.

tion has broadened to include Spam sonnets, limericks, and parodies like "The Spam of the Ancient Mariner" and "Spammerwocky."

SPAM Amusements

A sure cure for the rarefied air of the Spam Haiku Archive? Play an interactive Spam game. Spam Bowling allows you to "roll a ball" at a setup of ten Spam blocks wherever you position your cursor. Afterwards you can view the results, reset, and—"for added excitement"—reposition your cursor and try again. Find-the-Spam is another one-note joke, but if you know the joke, the fun's pretty much over. So we'll only say that playing the game inspired one visitor to muse, "Sometimes you just have to stop and smell the Spam," and another to remark, "It took . . .

SPAM BOWLING

time, but after some Zen training—What is the sound of one hand clapping? type of thing—I too found the Spam. Empty your mind."

After leaving your own deep thoughts about Find-the-Spam, you may want to surf on over and join the Great Spam Debate. You won't find a game at this site, but you will find an even larger body of Spam musings to which you can contribute. The predictable hodge-podge of derogatory comments about Spam ("tastes like a wet dog smells") and absurd alternative uses for it (wall spackle, canoe sealer) is occasionally punctuated by an insightful observation ("Spam is Caucasian soul food").

Gimme That SPAM-time Religion

There are also several Spam religious sites on the Internet. Surprising? Not really, argues Wes Robertson in the Webzine *Barbed Wire*. Spam shares "with God the twin attributes of omnipresence and a short, catchy name that also means something spelled backwards." So it's no wonder, he says, that Spam inspires religious awe.

To get an idea of just how much religious awe it inspires, visit the two biggest cybersites devoted to Spam worship. One of them, John's Shrine to Spam, opens with a Spam can flanked by two panels of stained glass, some bouncy electric organ music, and a warm welcome to the "weary Net traveler" looking for "the peace and tranquillity of Spam." Although the shrine also contains secular documents (such as the Python Spam sketch, Spam press clippings, and Spam recipes—including one for Spam wine), its main attraction is an archive of Spam religious texts that predate the commercial Internet.

John Swegan, a.k.a. Pastor Swiggy, "chief prophet of Spam."

John's Shrine to Spam

Yes, sacrilegious Spam cyberhumor seems to have gotten its start sometime in the early '70s, when several independent computer bulletin boards in Maryland chronicled the adventures of a group of Spam worshipers and their adversaries, the Force against Spam. The complete bible of these early Spammists and their Ten Spammandments are posted at John's shrine under the title "The Complete Spam." The bible, of course, begins with the book of Genespam in which Spod creates Spam, sees that it

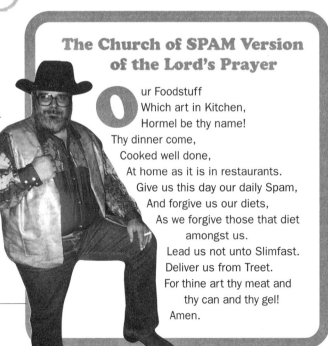

The Church of SPAM Version of the Lord's Prayer

Our Foodstuff
Which art in Kitchen,
Hormel be thy name!
Thy dinner come,
Cooked well done,
At home as it is in restaurants.
Give us this day our daily Spam,
And forgive us our diets,
As we forgive those that diet amongst us.
Lead us not unto Slimfast.
Deliver us from Treet.
For thine art thy meat and thy can and thy gel!
Amen.

The SPAM Legend

Long ago in a galaxy far away, a place called Minnesota to be exact, one of the great wonders of the universe emerged. The year? 1937. The wonder? The birth of Spam luncheon meat. At the time, the creator of the trademark Spam, J. C. Hormel, naturally had high hopes for his new offspring . . . but even he knew not what this tasty little treat could grow to be. Today Spam is the all-time, undisputed canned food icon of American culture. [It] is the talk of the Internet and the toast of the town (especially over whole wheat with lettuce, tomato and mayonnaise). All the while, the Spam legion grows . . .

—Spamtastic Catalog, No. 1

is good, and then in succession creates cans, can openers, and silverware.

John's Shrine to Spam is not officially affiliated with the Church of Spam, the other big Spam religious site on the Internet. However, it provides a link to the church and encourages visitors to continue on their "path to enlightenment" with Pastor Swiggy. A self-styled "espamgelist" and "chief prophet of Spam," Pastor Swiggy—also known as John Swegan—got his calling in the Church of Spam chat room of America Online. Shortly after his first visit, he became one of the room's principal participants and organizers. "The next thing I knew I was writing the Books of Spam," says Swegan, as if swept away by some divine force.

Swegan's writings are much more extensive than the Maryland tracts. They include prayers, sermons, tenets, and hymns (one with a sound bite of a bagpipe-accompanied solo that begins "Amazing Spam, how sweet thy gel") as well as over a hundred "Books of Spam" arranged in "volumes" of twenty books of twenty lines each. Most of the books are bawdy parodies of the

Bible. A passage from one of the few G-rated ones in "The Prophets of Spam" parodies biblical rhetoric while satirizing the Spam can opening system: "What can ye tell us of the Loop?" the crowd asks Spam prophet Thomas. "For we have heard that the Loop is bad, and it is of Slimfast!" Thomas answers, "Fear not. For the Loop was once the Key, and the Key was hard to use. And the children would take the Key whole and ingest it. And many met Spam before it was time. Now I am the Key and the Loop is the Ring. And the Ring has no beginning nor has it an end. . . . For the Loop is the Ring, for the Loop is the Key Ring."

Pastor Swiggy also offers his own version of the Ten Spammandments, which include "Thou shalt have no other meat by-product before Spam," "Honor thy father and mother with daily gifts of Spam," and "Remember the shopping day. May it be filled with Spam." Abide faithfully by these and the rest of the Spammandments and you will almost certainly go directly to "Hog Heaven" when you shed your container. "This will protect you," Pastor Swiggy says, "from spending an eternity in Gel . . . or any time at all in Porkatory."

The SPAMtastic Temple of SPAMmon

Although the Bible says you cannot serve both God and mammon, on the Internet you can serve both Spam and Spammon. After worshiping at John's shrine or Pastor Swiggy's church, just cybercruise on back to the official Spam site and order all the worldly Spam riches you can afford. You'll find Spam street signs, wall clocks, wristwatches, beach balls, umbrellas, straw hats, label pins, party packs, even glow-in-the-dark boxer shorts. You may also find the Spam Legend, a brief story of the luncheon meat's spectacular journey from simple sandwich meat to Internet icon. As Pastor Swiggy might say, Spod only knows what might come next.

GET SPAM STUFF

Acknowledgments

It only makes sense that great people would be attracted to a great luncheon meat. My work on this book proved it. Spam's goodness is reflected in the warmth, patience, and generosity of the people of Austin, Minnesota, who make it. For more than a week one snowy December and in hundreds of subsequent telephone conversations, the good people of Hormel Foods Corporation opened up their minds and their files to this pesky easterner. V. Allan Krejci, Meri Harris, Paulette Cummings, Gene Lifka, Jeff Grev, Jim Splinter, Richard Crane, Kevin Jones, and Peter Hoeper filled my plate with the most heapin' helpings of Spam information. To them and to such equally stellar examples of midwestern character as Tom Keating, Thomas and James Hormel, Marie Casey, Darryl Mickelsen, Tony Pierskalla, Tate Lane, and Helmer Peterson I owe my greatest debt of thanks, not to mention home-cooked Spam, bean, and pineapple casseroles.

If the people of Austin had the most to lose by trusting me with their Spam story, they also had something to gain. This was not true of the many Spam fans who fed me information and artwork, most especially David Arnsberger, Calyn Dougherty, Ruby Montana, and Dana Cox, organizers of the greatest independent charity Spam festivals held throughout our great land.

This work also owes a great debt to the Spam chefs and scholars that have gone before me, including Dorothy Horn, Ann Kondo Corum, Richard

Dougherty, and Doniver Lund. Dougherty's *In Quest of Quality: Hormel's First 75 Years* and Lund's *The Hormel Legacy: 100 Years of Quality* were particularly helpful for insights and information offered in Chapters 1 and 5, but no one should consider herself a serious student of Spam culture without reading the works of all four.

This book is filled with the names of people who generously shared their Spam stories. Here are the names of others who provided me with clippings or leads: Veronica "Aunt Rip" Van Ryn, Dell Sterling, Jeanne Kuehneman, Adele and Harold Blumenkrantz, Ormly Gumfudgin, Tom Robbins, Shelly Johnson, Gary Dryfoos, Martha Hirsch, Valerie Kraemer, Bill O'Grady, Abe Katz, Blair and Patty Moffett, Tom Climie, Carl Graham, Walter Callaway, William Leonard, Don Lewan, Keisling Lane, Pat Risser, Gloria Bickford, Dave Sigworth, Fran Fried, Walter Steiger, and Mika Chin; photographs, recipes, or research or editorial help: Viola and Douglas Wyman, Mia Malafronte-Luciano, Linda Beaulieu, Anna Dixon, Melanie Stengel, Susette Burton, Rebecca Carlson, Thom Duffy, Janet Hladky, Peggy Schenk, Kelly Degala, Ken Rabben, Mike Donovan, Jim Brogin, J. Roy

Parcells, Bob Pratte, George Synder, Doris Baldwin, Patricia Yeagle, Dolly Ammann, Steven Anders, Luther Hanson, Betsie Bolger, Cindy Cione, Allison Yuri Iwaoka, Al Jeffries, Sharon Jones of Global Shakeup Snowdome in Pasadena, California, and Marc Abrahams and the many Spam-savvy subscribers to his min-AIR Internet mailing list; and encouragement, advice, or space to write: Philip Blumenkrantz, Philip Greenvall, and Joyce Morral. For the chance to experience such evidence of care, everyone should write a book at least once in his life.

For a "take it easy" day-serve...

SPAM BEAN BAKE

Finally, I'd like to express my gratitude for an agent (John White) who always returns phone calls, a fellow writer (Judith Stone) who provided the (pork) link to a Spam-hungry editor, and a bookmaking team straight out of pig heaven. I speak specifically of designer extraordinaire G. B. D. Smith, and editors Kati Steele and Diane Sterling. Kati graciously cleaned the kitchen. Diane more than lived up to her last name. As an Austin, Minnesota, native, Diane had the vision to see that the world needed a book all about Spam and the smarts to know when to slice and dice, when to fry, and when to serve my words straight up. Royalties excepted, this book is truly hers as much as it is mine.

Illustration and Text Credits

Hormel Foods Corporation, Austin, MN. Copyright Hormel Foods Corporation. All Rights Reserved. Spam® is a registered trademark of Hormel Foods Corporation, Austin, MN. British Spam® material courtesy Newforge Foods, Ltd. All Rights Reserved: pages vii, ix, x, 1 background, 2, 3, 4, 6, 7, 8 top, 9, 15, 16 lyric, 17 bottom right, 18 top, 19 verse, 20 lyric, 21, 22, 24, 27, 30, 31 top right, 32, 33 bottom, 34, 36 top, 37, 38, 40, 41, 43 recipe, 48, 50 bottom, 53, 55 bottom, 57, 58, 59, 60, 61, 62, 63, 64, 65, 66 recipes, 67, 68, 69, 70, 71, 72, 73, 74, 75, 76, 77, 78, 79 top left, bottom, 80 top, 82, 83, 84, 85, 86, 92 recipe, 93 verse, 105 bottom, 110 recipe, 114, 115, 121 background graphics, 122, 124, 125, 128 bottom, 130, 132, 133 top, 134, 135.

Photo Larry S. Neilson: page ix.

Courtesy of DirectMark, L.L.C.: pages vii, 85 bottom right.

Hormel Historic Home, Inc.: page 5 top.

Arizona Republic/Phoenix Gazette. Used with permission. Permission does not imply endorsement.: page 5 bottom.

AP/Wide World: 26 top left, center, 31 top center, 85 left.

© Tribune Media Services. All Rights Reserved. Reprinted with permission.: pages 8 center, 31 bottom, 45 bottom, 97 top, 99 bottom, 100 top, 101 top.

© 1998 Hasbro, Inc. All Rights Reserved. Trivial Pursuit® and the distinctive design of the game board are registered trademarks of Horn Abbot Ltd. for the games distributed and sold in the U.S. under the exclusive license to Hasbro, Inc., © 1998 Horn Abbot Ltd. All Rights Reserved.: page 10 bottom.

Okay, so the name's funny.

National Archives: pages 18 bottom, 23 bottom right.

U. S. Army Signal Corps Photo: pages 19, 20 right, 24, 28 top.

Reprinted by permission: © 1945 The New Yorker Magazine, Inc. All rights reserved.: page 21 excerpt.

Howard Hovey: page 23 top.

Corbis: pages 25 bottom, 27 top, 27 bottom.

Hulton/Liaison: page 25 top.

Richard Ducker © 1943 from The New Yorker Collection. All Rights Reserved.: page 26 bottom.

Ralph Morse, Life Magazine © Time, Inc.: page 26 background image.

Joseph Gregoria: page 28 recipe.

Marvin W. Nye and courtesy of VFW Magazine, November 1947 issue: page 30.

Annals of Improbable Research, Cambridge, MA (altered wire service photo): page 31 top right.

© Original design by Kevin Pope. All Rights Reserved. Recycled Paper Greetings, Inc. Reprinted by permission.: page 33 top.

Photos by Sarra, from Hormel Archives: page 34.

Sonia Larson/Spamettes: pages 35 lyrics, 117 photo & lyrics.

Mr. Whitekeys, photo by Viola M. Wyman: page 42.

Randy Brandon/Third Eye Photography: pages 43 bottom, 44 left, 80 bottom.

Illustration by Blair Thornley: page 44 right.

Reprinted by permission of the Wall Street Journal © 1996 Dow Jones Company, Inc. All rights reserved worldwide.: page 45 left.

Austin Daily Herald file photos: pages 11, 36 bottom, 73 top.

D. J. Nordgren/ NMN, Inc.: page 12 top.

Illustrations by Frank Cummings: pages 12, 13, 14.

Lake County (Il.) Museum, Curt Teich Postcard Archives: page 14 top

Burt Plehal courtesy Hormel: page 15.

From Saturday Night at the Pahala Theatre copyright © 1993 by Lois-Ann Yamanaka. Published by Bamboo Ridge Press. First published in Bamboo Ridge: The Hawaii Writer's Quarterly. Reprinted by permission of Susan Bergholz Literary Services, New York. All rights reserved: page 45 poem.

Ann Kondo Corum: pages 46 recipe, 47 cartoon, 79 recipe.

Camera Hawaii: page 46.

Courtesy 7-11 Hawaii: page 46 ad slogan.

Pocholinga Productions: p. 46 lyric.

Photo Karen Hamada: page 47.

Stephen Craig: page 48 bottom right.

Anthony P. Bolante/TEAM SPAM OUTSIDE Online: page 49 bottom.

© 1998 Ann Summa: page 49 top.

Craig Yoder: page 50.

Bob Goliath Taich: page 51 top.

Lisa Heft: page 51 bottom.

Mike Seta/photo by James F. Brown: page 52 top.

Jeffrey Olson: page 52.

Global Shakeup Snowdomes, Los Angeles, www.snowdomes.com: page 53 snowdome.

Chuck Hudson: page 54.

Bisquick® is a registered trademark of General Mills, Inc.: page 65 top left.

Illustration courtesy of Mary Ann Smith, Bloomberg: page 80, right.

Dorothy Horn/Guam's Queen of Spam: pages 78 background image, 81, 93 recipe.

Richard Adams Associates design: page 86 bottom.

Shannon Wheeler/ cartoonist of Too Much Coffee Man: page 86 top right.

© Python (Monty) Pictures, Ltd.: pages 87, 88, 89, 124 graphics.

Archive Photos: page 89 top.

Louis Szathmary: page 90 recipes.